# THE GR

# RICHMOND

(revised and enlarged edition)

**John Cloake**

Richmond Local History Society
Paper No. 8

ISBN 0 9522099 0 X

First edition published by the Richmond
Society History Section as
Paper No 1, 1982
Reprinted 1985


New, revised and enlarged edition
published by the Richmond Local
History Society 1993

Printed by Castle Cary Press, Yeovil, SOMERSET

# FOREWORD

The origin of this publication lay in a lecture which I gave to the Richmond Society in February 1975, which led directly to the decision to found a History Section of the Society. In October 1981 I presented to the History Section a revised version of the same talk, which was then edited for printing as the Section's first published Paper.

In 1985 the Richmond Local History Society was formed as an independent society, and in agreement with the Richmond Society it took over all assets and publications of the History Section, which was then dissolved.

The demand for a short summary of Richmond's history has remained strong and, although *The Growth of Richmond* has been reprinted, stocks are now again exhausted. Over the years, however, my continued research has revealed a number of errors in the original publication. Moreover, readers' comments have suggested that the text should be expanded somewhat, beyond what it was possible to cover in a one-hour talk, especially to deal more fully with the nineteenth and twentieth centuries. This new edition is therefore not only fully revised, but it also contains a good deal of new material, corrected plans and some new illustrations. It is of course still only a very cursory glance at an extremely rich and interesting subject.

John Cloake
September 1992

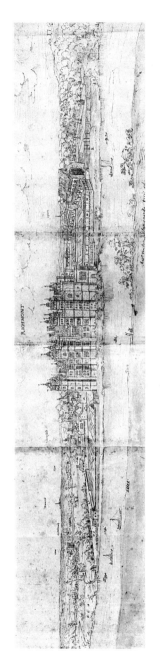

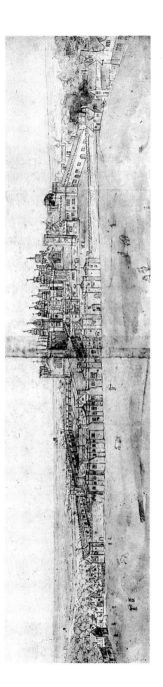

Richmond Palace in 1562. These two drawings by Anthonis van den Wyngaerde show the palace from the river (above) and from the Green (below) in its heyday. In the view from the river the abandoned chapel of the Observant Friary (and formerly of 'Byfleet') appears on the right; the tower of the Shene Charterhouse chapel can be seen in the background on the left. In the view from the Green it is interesting to note the houses already standing on the site of Old Palace Terrace and the end of King Street (left) and those, mostly built in the reign of Henry VIII, on the western corner of the Green (right).

*(Reproduced with permission of the Ashmolean Museum, Oxford)*

# THE GROWTH OF RICHMOND

Three Rs have determined the development of Richmond: Royalty, the River and the Railway. For much of its history, of course, there were only two. But Richmond owes its name to a king and its very existence to the royal house by the river. It was in 1501 that King Henry VII, having rebuilt the royal palace of Shene, largely damaged by a great fire four years before, decided to re-name it Richmond, after his earldom in Yorkshire. Gradually the village of Shene, around the Palace, adopted the new name.

But we should take a look first at Richmond's pre-history – the development of the royal manor of Shene. Shene is an Anglo-Saxon name meaning a place of shelter (not, as was long believed, "a shining place"). It is first mentioned in a historical document in the will of Theodred, Bishop of London, about 950 AD. Shene is not however mentioned in the Domesday Book; it was at that time a part of the royal manor of Kingston. In the early 12th century King Henry I divided Shene and Kew from the manor of Kingston to form the separate manor of Shene, which he granted to the Norman family of Belet.

The manor was subsequently divided into two halves and by the end of the 13th century one half was owned by Otto de Grandison, a Crusader, with the reversionary interest belonging to the Chancellor, Bishop Robert Burnel; the other half belonging to a Belet descendant, John de Valletort.

We have the first description of the property in inventories of the possessions of Burnel and de Valletort at their deaths in 1293 and 1301 respectively. Each held 200 acres of arable demesne land; the Burnel-Grandison portion also included 16 acres of meadow, a separate pasture, a warren (or reserved hunting ground) and a fishery as well as the main manor house itself with a garden, dovecote and park; the Valletort portion had 12 acres of meadow and a pasture on an island in the Thames called the Vineyard – additionally he had leased from Otto de Grandison a house and garden, 20 acres of arable and an acre of mead. There may have been originally more demesne land belonging to the manor than the 400 acres represented here, for there are a number of other 13th century references to freehold lands in Shene which do not tie in directly with the history of either half of the Belet inheritance; and lands and fisheries within the manor were granted to the great Priory at Merton. These included more meadows and a pasture ground of 16 acres in Kew and lands called "Priests" or "Merton Lands" in Shene itself. In addition to the demesne land were also the common fields.

It was just after the death of Bishop Burnel that Shene was first used as a royal court. Grandison appears to have rented the manor to Edward Prince of Wales in the 1290s. There are letters patent dated 1299 from Shene and from 1300 accounts survive of the household establishment of King Edward I there. In 1305 the King was there when he received in audience the commissioners he had sent to establish civil government in Scotland after his conquests, and in 1310 his successor Edward II was again holding court at Shene.

The manor had formally reverted to the Crown by 1313, when a new royal keeper of the manor was first appointed. A survey made of the manor at about this date gives details of the landholders, their holdings and the money rents and labour services which they owed to the Lord. There were altogether 14 free tenants, only six of whom held significant amounts of land, and 29 villein tenants owing labour services, five of whom were resident in the tiny hamlet of Kew. In all nearly 600 acres of arable land and just over 60 acres of meadow were in the hands of these manorial tenants. The arable land was in strips in the two large fields of Shene and in a separate smaller field at Kew. Between the fields and the river lay the demesne lands of the Lord and the open hunting warren.

In 1314 King Edward II established a house of Carmelite friars in the manor house of Shene, in thanksgiving for his escape after his defeat at Bannockburn. Two years later, however, he moved the Carmelites to a new home in Oxford. Then in 1327 the new King Edward III granted the manor of Shene to his mother Queen Isabella.

It was after Queen Isabella's death in 1358 that the manor house at Shene first began to assume the character of a palace. Edward III, who was evidently fond of the place, embarked on major works of improvement to turn it into a fitting royal home. The accounts for these works which continued for some 12 years at a cost of £2000 give us some idea of the palace as it stood by 1370. It was a moated house, with a great bridge over the moat leading to the main entrance gate, and another bridge (or jetty) towards the Thames, on each side of which a wharf was constructed. The buildings were part stone, part half-timber, with tiled roofs. There were two courtyards with fancy paving, the King's new apartments being in the inner one. Below the King's chamber was a cloister walk with another new chamber at the end of it. Both of these chambers had two fireplaces each; a huge room facing the garden had no fewer than eight fireplaces. There was a hall and a chapel. Two other main ranges of building contained: one of them, nine chambers "with latrines"; the other, the wardrobes of the King and the Queen and the chandlery. The main rooms were tiled and glazed. The King's chamber had a candelabrum in the shape of five roses. Outbuildings included large stables, a larder and kitchen, a roasting house and so on. Somewhere, there was a clock, which had a new belfry built in 1377. In the garden, or perhaps on that island called the Vineyard already mentioned, vines were planted. In the last two years of the King's reign, a great barn and a small hall were brought over from Wimbledon where they had been purchased intact, and were re-erected at Shene.

Edward III died in his palace at Shene in 1377. His grandson and successor, Richard II, made more improvements, including the tiling of the King's bath, additional apartments for the royal household, an improved jetty and steps to the water and the building of what must have been quite a large pavilion on the eyot in the river near the Palace – it is not surprising that we also hear of the purchase of a new barge and boat for the Palace.

Then, on 7th June 1394, came disaster. Richard's beloved Queen, Anne of Bohemia, died at Shene. Desolate, the King ordered the demolition of the Palace "as well the houses and buildings in the court within the moat and the court without the moat, as the houses and buildings in la Neyt beside the manor". Some of the materials were re-used at the Tower of London and some at the manor house of Sutton in Chiswick and at Windsor. The demolition was not however quite as complete as Richard had ordered, for there is evidence that the agricultural buildings in the outer court and also the royal gardens continued to be maintained.

For nearly 20 years, throughout the reign of Henry IV, Shene remained half-derelict. Then came a new lease of life. Henry V on his accession determined to rebuild, better and more splendid than before. The "King's great work" was started in 1414; and the first step was to make the Palace habitable by erecting prefabs. The timber manor house belonging to the King at Byfleet was completely demolished and re-erected at Shene on a new stone foundation on a site near to the ruined Palace, and much enlarged and embellished. The buildings included the King's ward and the Queen's ward, a chapel, a kitchen (surmounted by a great wooden carved figure of an antelope) and a bathhouse. By 1419 nearly £6000 had been spent on "Byfleet" – the name was retained. Meanwhile, on an adjacent site – between Byfleet and the site of the former Palace – work was started on the building of a new main Palace, which was however still incomplete when Henry died in 1422. Work was suspended until 1429 and then proceeded in fits and starts for a quarter of a century. Again we have many details of the work: of the antelopes and swans carved for the King's chamber, of the stained glass with designs of the royal arms and the King's beasts which went into the chapel, the great chamber and the privy chamber, of the panelling carved with divers beasts, "curiously wrought", in the chapel, of the lions and fleur-de-lys cresting of cornices and beams in the ceilings, of an oratory for the King over the porch of the hall, of new moats and garden walls and cloisters, of a new great quadrangle with gatehouse for the lodging of the King's household. We know about the master craftsmen and the materials – apart from the re-use of Byfleet, the manor house at Sutton was also cannibilized, stone came from Yorkshire and Devon, Oxfordshire and Normandy as well as from Kent and Surrey, lead and plaster from Lancashire, glass from London, bricks from Calais and from Petersham, trees for the garden from Rouen.

Alas, we have no picture of the Palace at this time – at least none identified as such. But I will hazard a speculation. The plan of the Tudor palace seems probably to have been almost identical with the Lancastrian one and it no doubt made use of the old foundations. In particular, the ground plan of the Tudor "privy lodgings" – that part facing the river which is the well known view – is reminiscent not of a Tudor house but of an early 15th century fortified manor house or castle. It bears a close resemblence to, say, Herstmonceaux built about 1440 – a square building with a central court and its outer walls embellished with many towers, and surrounded by a moat. That is what I see by the River Thames in, say 1450 – a residential but fortified castle like Herstmonceaux, linked by a bridge over the moat to two further courtyards like those of early colleges, and by the side towards the village a series of timber or half-timber buildings dominated by a chapel and by stone towers on the outer walls – the manor of Byfleet at Shene.

It was, I believe, the building of the new great quadrangle and gatehouse in the 1440s that brought the grounds of the Palace jutting forward onto the Green and, though houses were then built on the outside of the "Byfleet" wall facing the Green, a little piece of the Green

A model of the Charterhouse of Shene, designed by John Cloake for the Museum of Richmond. (The model was sponsored by Solaglas Ltd, whose offices in the King's Observatory adjoin the Charterhouse site.)

*(Reproduced with permission of the Museum of Richmond)*

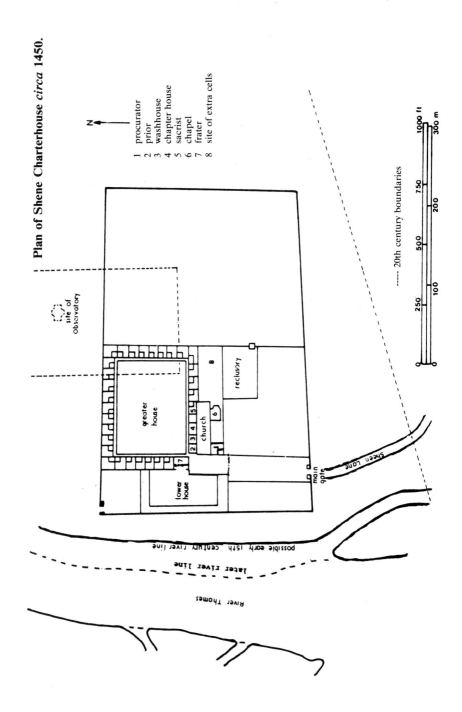

**Plan of Shene Charterhouse *circa* 1450.**

1 procurator
2 prior
3 washhouse
4 chapter house
5 sacrist
6 chapel
7 frater
8 site of extra cells

site of observatory

greater house

lower house

church

reclusory

main gate

Sheen Lane

possible early 15th century river line

later river line

River Thames

---- 20th century boundaries

was left extending past the corner of the Palace grounds. It still remains, at the end of King Street and Friars Lane.

The Palace was not the only feature of Henry V's "great work" at Shene. We are not apt to think of him as a pious man, but he had (at least when he had finished sowing his wild oats) a clear hankering after the life of the religious recluse. The Crusaders had brought to Europe knowledge of a different kind of religious life from that of the jolly and often corrupt congregation of monks – an eastern Christian tradition of the solitary hermit or anchorite. New orders were founded devoted to the contemplative life. Henry was much influenced by more than one such recluse. He was also carrying a burden of conscience. His father had been responsible for the deaths of Archbishop Scrope and of Richard II and had sworn in expiation to found three religious houses, but had died with his oath unfulfilled.

Henry determined to carry out his father's pledge. Where better to set to work on the building of new monasteries than in the royal lands at Shene and across the river in the royal manor of Twickenham and Isleworth? What better orders to favour for the three new houses than the hermitic Carthusians, the ascetic visionary Celestines and the contemplative Briggitines? The Celestine monastery at Isleworth proved abortive, and the Briggitines later moved from Twickenham Park to the Celestine site at Syon. But our concern is with the Carthusian monastery, the Charterhouse of Jesus of Bethlehem of Shene, the latest founded, largest and richest of all the English Charterhouses.

Where is it now? All trace above ground has vanished. It stood in the bend of the river north of the Palace and village of Shene, in what is now the golf course of the Mid-Surrey Club in the Old Deer Park, a little to the south-west of Kew Observatory. I have attempted, from documentary evidence, to reconstruct its plan.[1] Unlike most other monasteries, the cloister of any Carthusian Charterhouse contained rows of detached small houses, each with its own little walled garden - one for each monk. On the south side of the cloister was the church and chapter house. A second cloister to the west housed the lay brothers.

The building of the Shene Charterhouse went on concurrently with the work at Shene Palace, under a different master-mason, but under the general supervision of the Clerk and Comptroller of the King's

---

1   *See John Cloake: Richmond's Great Monastery: the Charterhouse of Jesus of Bethlehem of Shene, Richmond Local History Society Paper No 6, 1990.*

Works. The monastery was consecrated in 1415 and largely completed in two or three years thereafter. The materials were much the same as for the Palace, brick for some buildings, stone or part brick and part stone for some others, and almost certainly some lath and plaster timber-framed out-buildings, possibly on freestone foundations. Quite a lot of the materials came from the demolished royal manor house at Sutton. In 1416 Henry V additionally founded and endowed a separate reclusory within the precincts. Some further additions to the buildings were made in the later 15th century – new cells and an extra chapel for the church and a new conduit for extra water supply.

One other extra building was added later, in the reign of Henry VII. John Colet, the famous Dean of St Paul's, built himself a house within the precincts; and died there. Later Reginald Pole, the future Cardinal, lived in this house for a while in 1527-1529 and in 1530 it provided a temporary refuge for Cardinal Wolsey after his fall. Then Pole returned, and took up residence again for two years.

With the foundation of the Charterhouse and the rebuilding of the Palace came another change in the map of Shene. Large parts of what had been the royal hunting warren were granted to the Carthusians, first by Henry V, and subsequently by Henry VI and by Queen Elizabeth, consort of Edward IV. Also at about this time a new park was made beside the Palace; we are not sure where the park mentioned in 1293 was, but this one was on the northwest side of the Green and the Palace, roughly triangular in shape and adjoining the lands granted to the monastery. The first mention of this new park comes in 1437.

Little extra work seems to have been done on the Palace during the troubled years of the latter part of Henry VI's reign or those of the Yorkist kings. Edward IV granted Shene to his Queen, Elizabeth Woodville. It was reclaimed from her by her son-in-law Henry Tudor, Earl of Richmond, after he had become King as Henry VII. He started a programme of repair and new construction, but then at Christmas 1497, when he was at Shene with his court, came the disastrous fire which led to the decisions to rebuild the Palace almost completely – and then in 1501 to change its name to Richmond.

The appearance of the Tudor Palace can be judged from early pictures, the Wyngaerde drawings of 1562 (see p 4), the Fitzwilliam painting of c1625, Hollar's engraving of 1638. The many-sided window towers are similar to ones surviving from the same period at Windsor and at Thornbury Castle. We know most about it from the description given by the Parliamentary Surveyors in 1649, but I cannot forbear

Richmond Palace in the early part of Queen Elizabeth's reign: a model designed by John Cloake and built for the Museum of Richmond by Scale Link Ltd. (The model was sponsored by Crosby Associates (UK) Ltd).

*(Reproduced with permission of the Museum of Richmond)*

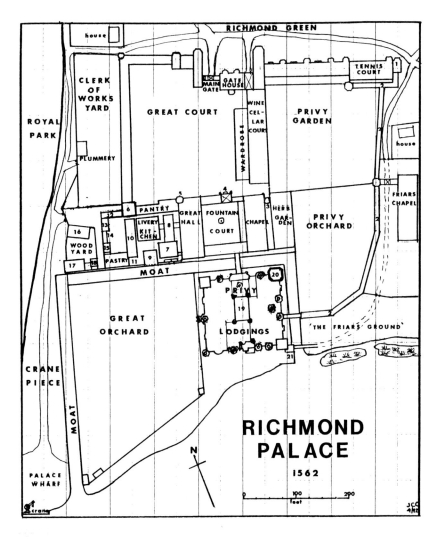

## RICHMOND PALACE

### 1562

KEY

| | | |
|---|---|---|
| 1 Banqueting house | 8 Cooks' lodgings | 15 Ale buttery |
| 2 Garden galleries | 9 House of office | 16 Woodyard lodging |
| 3 Bell tower | 10 Fish & flesh larders | 17 Coal store |
| 4 Middle gate | 11 Pastry Court | 18 Clerk of Woodyard |
| 5 Clock tower | 12 Poultry house | 19 Inner court |
| 6 Kitchen tower | 13 Scalding house | 20 'The Canted Tower' |
| 7 Privy kitchen | 14 Aumbry | 21 Watergate |

from quoting briefly from the lyrical account of an earlier visitor, Lancaster Herald, in 1501, when the rebuilding was just complete and the King was entertaining his new daughter-in-law, Katherine of Aragon:

"... This earthly and second Paradise ... the spectacle and the beauteous examplar of all proper lodgings, the King's goodly manor of Richmond, is set and built between divers high and pleasant mountains in a valley and goodly plains and fields where the most wholesome airs ... obtaineth their course and access; founded and erect upon the Thames' side ... he is quadrate and four square; girt and encompassed with a strong and mighty brick wall of great length ... beset with towers in his each corner and angle and also in his midway, of many grees and stages of height."

He goes on with four pages of glowing description.

Connected with Henry VII's rebuilding of the Palace was another new park. The King recovered from the Monastery of Syon lands on the other side of the river, enclosed them and made an extra park, known as the New Park of Isleworth or sometimes confusingly as "the New Park of Richmond in County Middlesex". This eventually became Twickenham Park.

The old buildings of the Byfleet manor at Shene, next to the rebuilt Palace, became the home of the last of Richmond's religious foundations. It was given by Henry VII to a Convent of Observant Friars, a branch of the Franciscan Order. Some extra work was put in on the buildings, to adapt them for their new occupants.

Let us now turn to the village and its fields. In the early 16th century the village of Richmond clustered between the Green and the western end of what is now George Street, stretching as far as the church, rebuilt between 1480 and 1510. Beyond the church was the royal "Grange". The Greens, both in Richmond and Kew, were larger than today. There were a few other buildings beside the Palace around the Green, some freehold and leased closes, including land belonging to Merton Abbey, granted for an endowment of the church and the priest's house, and others – among them the site of Old Palace Terrace – which belonged to Shene Charterhouse.

From what is now the corner of George Street and King Street, known as Four Elms, where stood the stocks, stretched the roads to Petersham: the old lower road and (because that was frequently flooded) the upper causeway that ran up Cutler's Hill to the great open space of

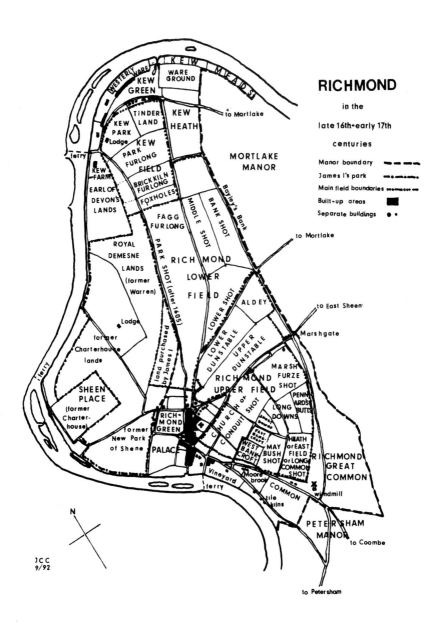

**RICHMOND**

in the

late 16th-early 17th

centuries

| | |
|---|---|
| Manor boundary | — — — |
| James I's park | — — |
| Main field boundaries | — — |
| Built-up areas | ■ |
| Separate buildings | ● ˙ |

WESTERLY WARE · KEW MEADS

KEW GREEN

WARE GROUND

to Mortlake

TINDER LAND

KEW PARK Lodge

KEW HEATH

KEW PARK FURLONG FIELD

MORTLAKE MANOR

KEW FARM

BRICK KILN FURLONG

EARL OF DEVONS LANDS

FOXHOLES

ferry

FAGG FURLONG

MIDDLE SHOT

BANK SHOT

Bayley's Bank

ROYAL DEMESNE LANDS (former Warren)

RICHMOND LOWER FIELD

to Mortlake

PARK SHOT (after 1605)

LOWER SHOT

ALDEY

to East Sheen

Lodge

former Charterhouse lands

land purchased by James I

LOWER DUNSTABLE

UPPER DUNSTABLE

Marshgate

MARSH FURZE SHOT

ferry

RICHMOND UPPER FIELD

PENNARDS BUTTS

SHEEN PLACE (former Charter-house)

CHURCH or CONDUIT SHOT

LONG DOWNS

RICH-MOND GREEN

former New Park of Shene

PALACE

EAST BANK CROFT

WEST BANK CROFT

MAY BUSH SHOT

HEATH or EAST FIELD or LONG COMMON SHOT

RICHMOND GREAT COMMON

Vineyard

Moores brook

COMMON

windmill

ferry

tile kilns

N

PETERSHAM MANOR

to Coombe

JCC 9/92

to Petersham

16

Richmond Common. Between Four Elms and the Ferry, there was some development; beyond it a major "close" or two, the rest – wasteland.

At Kew there were large parcels of land belonging to Merton Priory and to the Charterhouse. There were also a few houses near Kew Green, much longer then than it is today. The manorial meadows stretched along the riverside at Kew, north of the Green, and overlapped a part of the manor of Mortlake.

There were three main fields, Kew Field in the north, and the Lower and Upper Fields of Richmond. These were divided into "shotts" of various sizes, some of them with frequently changing names. The usual holding was what was called a "whole tenement" of 20 acres of arable, usually with an acre of meadow at Kew, and a "capital messuage" in the village for each such tenement. Sometimes the holdings were of half tenements (10 acres) and sometimes of two or more; but except for odd grants of bits of common land or of transfers of houses in the village, there are very few changes of ownership recorded in the early manor rolls which are not in terms of the 20 acre (virgate, as it was called) unit. This pattern persists well into Tudor times. Most of these 20 acre holdings were a conglomerate of separate acre and half-acre strips in the open fields, but a few (especially towards Kew and Mortlake) were of larger closes, even at times of 20 acres in a single contiguous parcel. These latter perhaps represent a later winning of arable land from the waste, while the strip-divided fields represent the original fields of the times of the Belets.

Throughout the 16th and early 17th centuries a creeping process of enclosure of the waste went on. Around the Greens, in both Richmond and Kew, along the roads, between the Petersham Road and the river, between the upper and lower causeways and between the upper causeway and the common fields, parcels of the waste were progressively granted to inhabitants and courtiers; and frequently we find, soon after, that they are described as "cottage newly erected on land late parcel of the waste" or some such formula. The Grange was split up and developed, the village spread a bit further east along the London Road and south along the Petersham Road. By 1620 King Street was almost fully developed with houses backing against the wall of the Friary; there was a continuous row of houses along the southeast side of the Green (but only about half the number there are today); Pensioners' Alley and Brewers Lane were intensively developed, as were two parts of the main street round the Red Lion Inn and the Parish Church. Beyond were scattered large houses and cottages. At Kew there

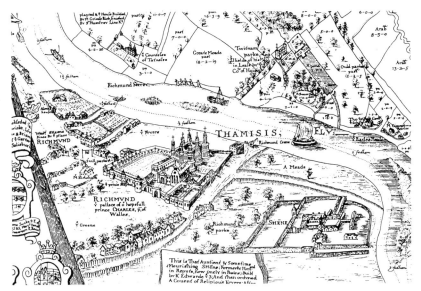

Richmond in 1635, showing the Charterhouse, now 'Sheen Place' (right), the Palace (centre) and part of the town around the Green and towards the ferry. A detail from Moses Glover's map of Isleworth Hundred at Syon.

*(Reproduced with permission of His Grace the Duke of Northumberland)*

were three or four large houses, and some dozen cottages north and south of the Green.

The mid-16th century was one of the two high spots in the history of Kew, which suddenly became the seat, not of kings but of king-makers. At the beginning of the century much of the property in Kew was owned by one Thomas Byrkis, but in 1509 estates there were acquired from him by Sir Charles Somerset, a second cousin of Henry VII, who was captain of the Yeomen of the Guard, and was later created Earl of Worcester. Another house and lands at Kew were granted to Somerset by King Henry VIII in 1517. By consolidating his holdings, Somerset (or possibly his son) was able to make a small Kew Park of 19 acres, in which was built a hunting lodge. This, and another house, roughly opposite across the western end of the Green, by the riverside, which Somerset bought from one Richard Blacket, remained in the Somerset family for two more generations, then passed through several hands before coming, in 1587, into the possession of Dr William Awberry. Somerset also built a large new mansion by the riverside, which was later bought by Charles Brandon, Duke of Suffolk, Henry

VIII's brother-in-law, and became known as Suffolk Place. It was demolished in the 1560s. The daughter of Charles Brandon and Princess Mary was Frances, who married Henry Grey, created Duke of Suffolk after Brandon's death – the parents of the ill-fated Lady Jane Grey.

Another house in Kew, Kew Farm, was acquired from Anthony Byrkis, the son of Thomas, in 1534 by Henry Norrys, an "esquire of the Body" to Henry VIII. This house had attached to it the original chapel of Kew, licensed by the Bishop of Winchester in 1522 as a private chapel for Thomas Byrkis. Norrys was implicated in the accusations against Anne Boleyn and executed in 1536. His house was granted to Sir Edward Seymour, later Duke of Somerset, the brother of Henry VIII's third wife Jane and uncle and "Protector" of Edward VI. From him it passed to Sir John Dudley, the Lord High Admiral, and subsequently to two successive owners, Sir Miles Partriche and Sir Henry Gate, both in turn involved in plots against the throne and attainted.

Eventually the house and its grounds came back to the Dudleys, together with lands and a house which had belonged in the late 15th century to the Courtenay Earls of Devon – another much executed family, which had the misfortune to carry Plantagenet blood and the resulting tendency to be implicated in plots and to lose and regain their lands and titles again and again. These possessions also passed through a series of hands in the later part of Elizabeth's reign, including one Thomas Gardiner, a teller of the Exchequer, whose tenure was abruptly terminated when it was found that he was £24,000 in arrears with his accounts! Eventually, towards the end of the century, they and the Suffolk lands all passed into the hands of the Portman family. There let us leave them, to return later, while we look at the other major change in the map of the 16th century.

This was the result of the dissolution of the monasteries. In Richmond the first to go, in 1534, was the house of Observant Friars. Strong adherents of Queen Katherine, and resolutely opposed to the King's divorce, they were no longer welcome neighbours for the Palace. Their warden was executed in April 1534; and the entire order of Observant Friars was suppressed in the summer of that year, some to go to the Tower and some dispersed to live in confinement in other monasteries. The Friary fell into disrepair. In one of Wyngaerde's drawings of the Palace in 1562 the chapel can still be seen, but it must have been demolished soon after. The site was leased out to a succession of private tenants.

The great Charterhouse survived only a little longer. Though its Prior (from 1535) was a complaisant character, who tried to ingratiate himself with Thomas Cromwell, in sharp distinction to the Prior and monks of the London Charterhouse who suffered martyrdom rather than accept the King as head of the Church, Shene suffered dissolution early in 1538.

As happened with many of the suppressed monasteries, Shene and its immediately adjacent lands were promptly granted to one of the great nobles – Edward Seymour, then Earl of Hertford, soon to become the Protector Somerset, already a resident of Kew. He started to turn it into a private residence, under the name of Sheen Place. When he was attainted and executed in 1551, it was granted to Henry Grey Duke of Suffolk. When the latter, with his neighbour Northumberland, now proprietor of Syon across the river, had plotted to put their children Jane Grey and Guilford Dudley on the throne, it was to their house at Sheen that the Grey family – such as were left unimprisoned – were sent. Suffolk and his daughter were finally executed in 1554 after Sir Thomas Wyatt's rebellion, and Queen Mary gave the house back to Somerset's widow.

Mary's accession was the signal for some of the braver English Carthusians (who had taken refuge at Bruges) to attempt a comeback, led by Father Chauncey of the London Charterhouse. Befriended by that Shene "old boy" Cardinal Pole, now Archbishop, and by Sir Robert Rochester, Controller of the Queen's Household and a brother of one of the martyrs of the London Charterhouse, they were successful. Mary, as soon as she could get it back from the very reluctant Duchess of Somerset, gave them Shene as a place to refound their order. Rochester helped, financially and administratively, with the rebuilding, but died a year later. One year later still, in November 1558, Cardinal Pole and Queen Mary died on the same day. Some of the brethren of Bruges had warned Chauncey against undue optimism: "Quicker than you look for you will be hurled suddenly from your buildings." The second dissolution rapidly followed Elizabeth's accession and in July 1559 the monks were expelled from Shene back to Flanders where they formed an exiled community called "Sheen Anglorum".

Elizabeth restored the building to the Duchess of Suffolk. After her death in November 1559, Sheen Place was rented for nine years by the Sackville family. It was granted to Sir Thomas Gorges and his wife Helen Marchioness of Northampton in 1584, on condition that all but the Prior's House should be made available for lodging the Queen's officers when she stayed at Richmond Palace. For some 60 years the western part of the site was used as the Palace stables.

When Elizabeth died in the Palace in 1603 and James I moved in, one of his first moves was to set an example which was followed, disastrously, by his son some 30 years later. He made another new Richmond Park. Most of it consisted of former Charterhouse lands, reclaimed from Gorges, to which were added the old "New" Park, some extra land that had remained in the royal demesne, and – by purchase – some 35 acres of land from the Richmond fields north of the Green. This remained the "New Park" until Charles I made his New or Great Park, when James's enclosure became the Old or Little Park, today the Old Deer Park (and part of Kew Gardens).

In the new Park, King James had a new Lodge built in 1605/6 – a small mansion built on the old H-plan. It was to become, a hundred years later, the nucleus of a new royal home in Richmond.

King James's Park did not include the walled monastery site itself. This was left as an island of leased Crown-owned residential property; it preserved the name of "West Sheen" until 1769 when the last outstanding lease fell in and the Crown resumed full possession. The remaining houses were demolished; and in 1771 the final traces – the outer walls and the gates – also disappeared.

The Tudor Palace stood, and was embellished and improved, from the reign of Henry VII until after the execution of Charles I. King Henry VIII briefly allowed Wolsey to use it when the latter had presented him with Hampton Court, and Wolsey too spent money on it. But when he fell finally from favour it was to the lodge in the old park that he returned for a few weeks before seeking sanctuary in the Charterhouse. Later Henry VIII granted the manor to Anne of Cleves. For much of the rest of the Tudor period, the manor was farmed out on lease, but the Palace itself and its park were specifically retained for royal use. Queen Elizabeth used it frequently, and died there.

Under the Stuarts, Richmond became the seat of the Prince of Wales. James I's eldest son Prince Henry lived there, and after his death, Prince Charles. Prince Henry had great plans for rebuilding the Palace and for redesigning the gardens. Solomon de Caux, the great French landscape gardener, started to design new grottoes and artificial mountains and giant figures for the gardens and the riverside; and the young Inigo Jones was responsible for reclaiming some extra land from the river in front of the Palace. With Prince Henry's death these projects came to an end.

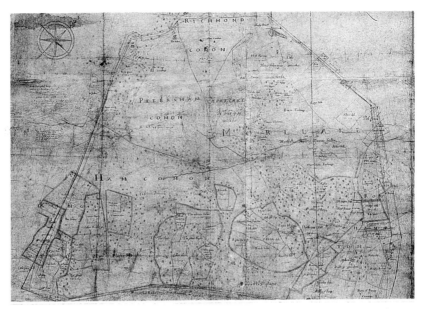

Nicholas Lane's plan of the lands to be enclosed in Richmond Park shows several earlier proposed boundaries as well as the line of wall finally determined.

*(Reproduced with permission of the Museum of London)*

Charles I built up his great collection of pictures partly at Richmond. He created the fourth "new" Richmond Park in 1635. He compulsorily purchased and enclosed many private estates, a significant part of the Mortlake common field and much of the common land of Richmond, Petersham, Ham, Kingston, Mortlake and Putney. Although the sums paid out in compensation were generous, this was one of the arbitrary acts held against Charles I. The story is told that Charles II, also anxious to make a new park, asked a minister what it would cost. "Only a crown, Your Majesty," the minister replied. But we can today be grateful to Charles I. If he had not enclosed the Park it would almost certainly by now be built on.

Then came the Civil War. Richmond was prepared to receive Charles, as a prisoner, shortly before his execution, but he was sent instead to Hampton Court. When Parliament determined to sell off Crown property, the Parliamentary Surveyors catalogued the Palace with their customary thoroughness; and it was sold in 1650 for some £10,000. The main buildings – the Privy Chambers, the Hall, and the

Chapel – were rapidly demolished and the materials used for other houses in Richmond. The rest was carved up into a series of separate dwellings. When the Surveyor General of Crown Lands looked at the wreck in 1660 after Charles II's restoration, he noted its division into some 25 separate properties, several of them occupied or claimed by a Mr Henry Carter who was, in another document, described as "the first puller down of the King's house" and who was alleged to have made over £2000 from the sale of the stones and materials. (The Manor Court complained that carts, loaded with stone, were ruining the Green.) It is hardly surprising to find that Mr Carter had raised forces to oppose the Restoration! Another despoiler of the royal property was John Bentley, formerly the King's woodmonger, alleged to have made £20,000 from cutting down and selling the trees in the royal parks. Bentley got away with it, and built, from the proceeds, a large house lying between the corner of the Green and the royal bakehouse by the Park Gate on the northwest side of the Green, to which he was able to attach the ground behind – once Henry VI's "New Park", which briefly became known as "Bentley Park". It then became the grounds of the new mansion built by Sir Charles Hedges, Secretary of State, in the 1690s – subsequently owned in turn by Sir Matthew Decker, Viscount Fitzwilliam, and the Earls of Pembroke.

By 1660 the Palace was too far gone for any normal restoration. James II, to whom it was granted as Duke of York in 1664, was presented with a design for a new palace by the architect of Les Invalides in Paris, Liberal Bruand, but never proceeded with it. Instead, in 1688 he got his Clerk of Works, Christopher Wren, to start on some work of renovation of the Wardrobe and Gate House, which was however promptly stopped when James went into exile. But for the most part the division of the remaining old buildings was accepted and regularized after the Restoration in 1660, and Crown leases granted for the subdivided properties. One can follow their gradual rebuilding and the slow disappearance of the kitchen courts and the original battlemented outlines right through the 18th century. First to go was the northeast corner, replaced by Tudor Place, then the Middle Gate building was rebuilt as Trumpeters' House, and the northwest section of the front wall as Old Court House and Wentworth House; to be followed by a major section of the rest of the front wall as four terrace houses for the Princess of Wales' Maids of Honour in 1724-25. A big new house sprang up in the 1740s by the riverside – the mansion of the Earl of Cholmondeley, and later of the Duke of Queensberry. Later came another landmark, which still happily survives. On the Palace wharf, at the end of Old Palace Lane, a brewhouse built about 1700 was replaced in 1758-60 by Asgill House.

During the 17th century the process of encroachment on the commons and Greens continued, until by the end of the century most of the land now developed had been granted into private hands. One grant of particular interest was that of an acre of land on the Great Common in 1621, on which a windmill was to be built. This stood roughly on the site of the Richmond Gate Hotel near what was soon to become the gate of Richmond Park. It can be seen in one of the early 18th century paintings of Richmond, but it disappeared about 1725. New cottages and some new large houses sprang up along the roads to Petersham and to London.

The prosperity of Richmond in the mid-17th century can be judged from hearth tax returns of 1664. Of the 263 houses in the village only ten had but a single hearth – the norm for the average agricultural labourer in poorer areas. Two-thirds had more than two hearths, nearly one-half had five or more, and nearly a quarter had eight or more, which certainly brings them into the category of substantial mansions. Ten houses in Richmond had more than 16 hearths. At Kew there were only 29 houses altogether – but a higher proportion both of very big ones and of small cottages.

In houses on the Town Hall and Castle Hotel site lived for a few years "the Leicestershire connection" – the local Wright family had married, in two generations, into the Farnhams of Quorn. Next door to them came to live the Farnhams' Leicestershire neighbour Sir William Herrick of Beaumanor, the King's jeweller and banker. Herrick also held a lease of Moorebrook, a house and estate of 11 acres on the Hill, between the upper and lower roads to Petersham, above Compass Hill – the area where medicinal springs were discovered in the 1670s.

These springs were to be developed as the basis of a spa and pleasure gardens. I doubt if the waters were all that good; but they served to initiate the development of Richmond Wells, opened in 1696, as a place of entertainment. There are many advertisements in the early-18th century for concerts and dancing at the Wells, but their popularity faded by mid-century – and they became a centre of rowdyism and a nuisance to the local inhabitants. They were finally bought up in 1763 by the Misses Houblon (who lived in what was later called Ellerker House and which became in 1809 the gothic castle on the Hill) and the site was redeveloped with houses for the nobility – Cardigan House and Lansdowne House. Nearby, on the Hill, the first Richmond theatre was opened in 1718 in a former barn. It was replaced the next year by a theatre converted from a stable of "Scott's Royal Ass House" – the "self-drive hire" establishment of that age – but this theatre died with its proprietor in 1725. Five years later a new, purpose-built "playhouse" was opened just above the corner of the Vineyard. But as the Wells fell out of fashion, so did the theatre on the Hill. In 1765-66 the new Theatre Royal was built on the corner of the Green by Old Palace Lane.

Another development of the 17th century was the building of almshouses. The first were called Queen Elizabeth's, founded by Sir George Wright in 1600 and built on the Petersham Road just south of Ferry Hill. They were followed by Bishop Duppa's on the Terrace in the mid-17th century. In 1695 Michel's almshouses were founded, built in the Vineyard – where they were later rebuilt and joined in the 18th and 19th centuries by both the earlier foundations removed from their original sites.

The Vineyard is rather a puzzle. I have mentioned the name as belonging to an island in the Thames in 1301. In Tudor and Stuart times however, the "Vineyard" was the name of a close of land south of Ferry Hill between the river and the Petersham Road. The street we know today as the Vineyard is described as the "lane leading to the Vineyard". Yet in the 18th century, there was another piece of ground, just by the bend in the road at the Halford Road-Onslow Road corner, which was called "Stanley's Vineyard", where Vineyard House was built in the early-18th century.

Mention of the Vineyard brings us back to the town fields. In the early part of the 17th century most of the transfers of land in the fields were still in blocks of whole tenements of 20 acres or half tenements of 10, but a breaking-up process was beginning. There are increasing sub-divisions – an acre here, a couple of acres there (often in four separate half-acre strips) – split off from the main holding. In 1620, when a list of the holders of land in the fields was compiled, only 12 persons between them still held over 80 percent of the land, but there were some 40 others with holdings of less than 10 acres, 25 of whom had only two acres or less. The splitting up continued, but towards the end of the 17th century a new process can be seen emerging – the exchange of strips to consolidate larger holdings in one place. And a new type of manor tenant appears in significant numbers – the London merchants, who built houses on the little estates made up from

Above: The Terrace, the windmill and the park gate c1720. On the far left is the Roebuck tavern; the pair of tall houses are Nos 1 and 2 The Terrace, built c1700. The smaller house adjacent to them is No 3 The Terrace, built c1697, as it was when it was the home of William Hickey. Opposite, by the end of the terrace walk, is the group of cottages which included the Bull's Head tavern and which were replaced by The Wick in 1775. A detail from a painting by Leonard Knyff, 1650-1722.

*(Reproduced with permission of Spink & Son Ltd)*

Below: Michel's Almshouses in the Vineyard, founded in 1695. A detail from a drawing and plan made by John Pullen in 1716.

*(Reproduced with permission of the London Borough of Richmond upon Thames)*

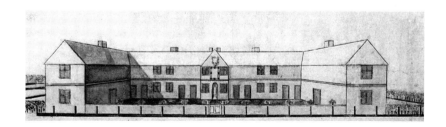

consolidated holdings in the fields. Typical examples are Felix Stokes and Nathaniel Rawlins, members of the Haberdashers Company of London. By purchase and exchange in the 1690s Stokes acquired a holding of two or three contiguous acres at the western end of Church Shott, between the Vineyard and Red Lion Street. On the middle of the land, by a footpath leading to Ferry Hill, stood a barn or cottage; one other cottage stood by Red Lion Street. In 1695 Rawlins purchased this land from Stokes and bought some additional adjoining property. At the top of this estate he built a new house for himself, which still stands – Clarence House in the Vineyard. We know he was building it in 1696, for he diverted the footpath leading up the hill from the church to give himself a better forecourt and was fined by the Vestry for doing so (which is why there is still a bend in Patten Alley). Having done this, he pulled down the old house in the middle of the land and in its place built a pair of gabled houses – perhaps unique for the period in being a mirror-image semi-detached pair (built back-to-back rather than side-by-side). They too still stand – the Rosary and the Hollies in Ormond Road. The forecourt of the Unitarian Church was their stable yard. In all, Rawlins acquired some 10 or 12 houses in Richmond, including some built by one John Drew.

John Drew was also a new type of figure on the Richmond scene, though he came of an old established Richmond family. The son of a bricklayer, he called himself "architect" – but was in reality a speculative builder. There were many other examples at the end of the 17th and the beginning of the 18th century: for instance, Michael Pew, who built the original houses on the sites of 1, 2 and 3 the Terrace and houses on Kew Green; and John Price, who developed the area round Little Green and the end of Parkshot. They would buy up old cottages or empty sites, mortgage them, build a new house on part of the site, mortgage or sell that, build another next door, and so on. This was one of the typical ways in which parts of Richmond developed apace in the early 18th century.

Two large speculative developments of the 1690s were financed by rich Londoners: one was the building of Old Palace Terrace and Paved Court; the other was the construction of Heron (originally "Herring") Court, with three large houses by the riverside and a terrace of five smaller houses facing Hill Street.

Now the town was really beginning to spread – up the hill and on the Terrace, along the lane behind the church, around the village pond at the end of George Street (where Dome Buildings now stand in an area then called "World's End"), around the Green and up the roads leading towards Kew, Mortlake and Marshgate, even two or three houses at Marshgate itself, and another concentrated but isolated development around the Green at Kew. In the early 18th century a few more scattered large houses were built in Church Shott – Halford House, Vineyard House, Mount Ararat for instance – and for the first time some built-up roads were developed on land which had been part of the fields – Church Terrace for example – and Ormond Row – the latter named for the popular local figure, James Butler, Duke of Ormonde.

The Duke, one of the great men of the early 18th century, Marlborough's successor as Commander in Chief of the British army in the reign of Queen Anne, married to the Queen's niece, obtained in 1704 a grant of the Lodge in Richmond Old Park – the house built in 1605, but which had recently been renovated by William III as a hunting lodge. Ormonde substantially rebuilt and enlarged the house, now formally know as Richmond Lodge. In 1715 he espoused the Jacobite cause, was impeached and attainted in absentia (having sought refuge in France) and his lands were forfeited to the Crown. Although Ormonde's brother was permitted to retain Richmond Lodge, his interest in it was soon acquired by the Prince of Wales. Royalty returned to Richmond as residents, and the Lodge soon became the favourite home of the future George II and his wife Caroline. Caroline had the northern part of the grounds laid out in landscaped gardens by Charles Bridgeman, one of the pioneers of the new informal school, with pavilions (including a "Hermitage" and "Merlin's Cave") built by the architect William Kent.

George II commissioned at least two designs for a new palace to replace the Lodge, but never proceeded with them. When George III came to the throne, he did the same. Plans were prepared this time by Sir William Chambers, and to improve the views from the new palace the last buildings on the old Charterhouse site were demolished in 1770-71. But the King ran short of money and work proceeded only very slowly. Then in 1772 the King's mother Princess Augusta died and George decided to move instead into her house at Kew. The work on the new palace was abandoned; and the old Lodge was pulled down. The only new building that had actually been put up was the King's Observatory, built by William Chambers in 1769, to enable the King, a keen astronomer, to observe the transit of Venus that year.

We left the history of the big houses in Kew at the beginning of the

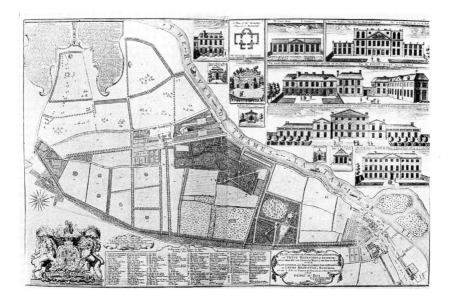

Richmond Gardens and the royal residences at Richmond and Kew – John Rocque's plan published in 1734. The south elevation of the King's 'Richmond Lodge' appears at the top right; its north elevation, with the adjacent stable block, is on the line below. The difference in style is due to the new south front built for the Duke of Ormonde c1710-15; the northern side reveals more of the old house built for James I as renovated and enlarged for William III. The third and bottom lines show Frederick Prince of Wales's 'White House' at Kew. Here again the two elevations are strikingly different, and it seems probable that the north side (bottom line) was largely incorporated from the existing Kew House when William Kent reconstructed it for Frederick in 1731-35. The central building in the top line is the orangery of Richmond Lodge (by Kent). At the left of the top line is the 'Queen's House', pulled down to make way for George III's 'Gothic' palace at Kew. Next to it is a plan (and below that, an elevation) of the Hermitage, by Kent. Four other small garden buildings are also shown.

17th century, in the hands of the Portman and Awberry families. The house in Kew Park passed from Morgan Awberry to Sir Arthur Gorges in 1605 and from Gorges' son to Sir Richard Bennett, a city merchant and nephew of Sir William Herrick, in 1634. Bennett purchased substantial additional lands from his neighbours, so that his property extended alongside the Old Park of Richmond. On his death it passed to his daughter Dorothy, wife of Sir Henry Capel, brother of the Earl of Essex. Capel was a passionate gardener, and laid out the grounds, built greenhouses and introduced many rare plants and trees. Dorothy Capel continued to live there long after her husband's death, but when she died in 1721 the house descended to her great niece Elizabeth, wife of Samuel Molyneux, secretary to the Prince of Wales. His great interest was astronomy and he converted the east wing of the house into an observatory. After Molyneux's death, his widow (who caused a scandal by eloping with the doctor on the very day her husband died) gave a lease of the house to the new Prince of Wales, Frederick, who thus established himself as a neighbour of his royal parents in Richmond.

Frederick and his wife Augusta were keen botanists and gardeners. To the original grounds of the "White House" (as it was called after it had been largely rebuilt by William Kent) Frederick added more land by lease and purchase of the last remains of the Kew Field and the northern end of Park Shott in the Lower Richmond Field. Close to the house a special botanical garden was laid out. The plans which Frederick had for embellishing his grounds were brought to a stop by his death in 1751, but Augusta, who continued to live in the White House, then employed Sir William Chambers to lay out "Kew Gardens" and to adorn them with a multitude of ornamental buildings, of which only the Orangery, the Pagoda and a few classical temples now remain. Hardly had Chambers finished his work at Kew when George III engaged Lancelot ("Capability") Brown to redesign his "Richmond Gardens" next door.

After Augusta's death in 1772 George III and Queen Charlotte moved into the White House, enlarged for them by Chambers, and this (though still leased from the Capel family) now became the principal royal seat in the area.

Meanwhile the royal estate in Kew had been variously expanded. One of the houses owned by the Portmans in the early 17th century had been sold by Sir William Portman in 1630 to a merchant named Samuel Fortrey. He rebuilt the house in 1631 in the fashionable "Dutch" style. It remained in the hands of his descendants until 1697 when it was sold to Sir Richard Levett, Lord Mayor of London in 1700, whose daughter in due course leased it to Queen Caroline who used it as a royal nursery. It then became the house of Amelia the Princess Royal. By the 1770s it was being used for another generation of royal children – George III's; and in 1781 it was purchased by the Queen. The King and Queen moved there when the White House was demolished in 1802, and it inherited the name "Kew Palace". George III's last visit was in 1806, but the Queen stayed there occasionally until her death in 1818. From then it remained virtually unused for 80 years until Queen Victoria opened it to the public in commemoration of her Diamond Jubilee. Kew Gardens and the northern part of Richmond Gardens were taken over officially by the state in 1841 as the Royal Botanic Gardens.

The largest of the Portman houses at Kew, Kew Farm, which stood by the river to the southwest of the Dutch House, had been taken over by the Earl of Ancrum and enlarged into a great mansion. At the end of the 17th century this was replaced by two smaller houses, but the estate still had extensive lands contiguous with the north of Richmond Gardens. This whole estate was leased by Queen Caroline in the 1730s. One of the houses, facing the tip of Kew Green, became known as "the Queen's House". The other, to the south of it, was occupied by the Mistress of the Robes – and later by the governess of George III's daughters. These properties were all finally purchased by Queen Charlotte in 1781. Some of the other houses around Kew Green, close to the royal estate, were also bought up by the royal family and, after occupation by royal dukes, were eventually attached to Kew Gardens. In 1802 the King was finally able to purchase the White House and its grounds.

George III still hankered after the idea of a new palace. In 1800 he commissioned James Wyatt to build a small palace in the fashionable Gothic style on the site of the Queen's House at Kew. The White House, the Queen's House and its neighbours were pulled down. Slowly a massive pile rose by the side of the Thames. By 1806 it was virtually complete externally, but not yet finished inside. But by 1806 the King was growing blind, and suffering increasingly frequent bouts of his "madness". In 1811 the Prince Regent finally brought the works to a halt. The castle stood empty and unfinished until it was demolished in 1828. Some of the materials were salvaged and reused and the rest blown up. It was an interesting and pioneer building, despite its archaic garb, for all the load was carried on cast iron columns and iron plate arches. The plan consisted of a courtyard, surrounded on three sides

The development of Richmond Hill: two views, of c1740 (anonymous) above, and of c1805 (by J. I. Richards) below. The earlier drawing shows on the right the original Star and Garter tavern built in 1738. Beyond it lies the gate of the park, adjoining which are two houses on the present site of Ancaster House. The left hand one was shortly after enlarged to become the Duke's Head tavern. On the far left is a house and coachhouse on the site of the Richmond Gate Hotel. The view of c1805 shows on the right The Wick (1775) and beyond it Wick House (1772) and the Star and Garter's new building of 1803. To the left is Ancaster House (1772) and the new park gate (1798).

*(The Richards painting is in a private collection and is reproduced by permission)*

by battlemented office buildings and leading on the fourth side to a residential block with a grand staircase and the state apartments, liberally adorned with turrets and with a central tower dominating the whole.

This century of renewed royal presence in Richmond and Kew gave a strong stimulus to the development of houses for the court and aristocracy. The area of Richmond and Twickenham, with its river, its clean air, and its convenience to London – only a two hour journey by coach – became a centre for what one might call weekend cottages or summer houses, though they were usually substantial villas. All along the riverside, and on Richmond Hill with its renowned view, and on the eastern edge of the town, sprang up comfortable houses – large by present standards – but small in comparison to the great country seats.

This process reached a peak in the 1770s, when, following the closure of Richmond Wells, the area at the top of Richmond Hill was rapidly developed. The Terrace itself was laid out afresh in 1775. Ancaster House, the Wick, Wick House, Downe House all rose within a decade, while the existing Doughty House and 3 The Terrace were rebuilt and embellished. So was the Star and Garter Inn, which now embarked on its career as one of the most fashionable hotels in the vicinity of London. Between Richmond Hill and the River, Cardigan House, Lansdowne and Buccleuch Houses and several others were also built at this time.

This growth of Richmond as a resort for the fashionable brought new prosperity to the village. Many new ale houses and coffee houses were opened and new hotels built. Much rebuilding went on in the centre and around the Green, and at Kew, and on the eastern and southern fringes of what was fast becoming a small town. At the end of the 18th century an influx of French émigrés brought a new cosmopolitan flavour to the local society.

Villas also sprang up all along the Twickenham bank of the river, and this bank became even more conveniently situated for access to the court at Richmond and Kew when the river was finally bridged at Richmond in the 1770s.

A wooden bridge had been built at Kew in 1758, and there was much interest subsequently in plans to build a bridge at Richmond to replace the old ferry. A great controversy arose over the siting. The main entrepreneur was the proprietor of the ferry and he wanted to build the bridge at the foot of Ferry Hill, where it would link up with the existing road through Twickenham Meadows. The inhabitants, who had

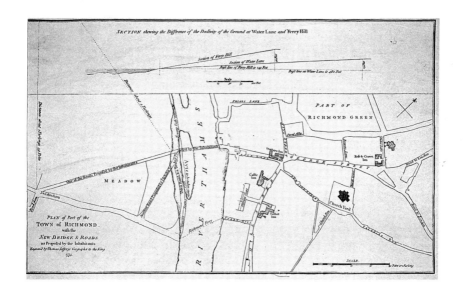

Above: The controversy over the siting of Richmond Bridge. The plan shows the site at the end of Water Lane proposed by the inhabitants of Richmond in 1773, with alternative access routes on the Twickenham side. The diagram at the top makes the point that the slope down Water Lane is much easier as an approach route than the steep Ferry Hill.

Below: James Paine's design for Richmond Bridge, as executed on the Ferry Hill site and completed in 1777. (The second tollhouse at the Twickenham end was omitted in construction.)

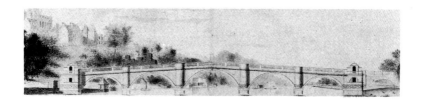

suffered since time immemorial from the awkward access to the ferry due to the steepness of Ferry Hill, wanted a bridge but a change of site. They wanted the old Water Lane widened as a continuation of George Street and a bridge built there. But the owner of the estates on the Twickenham side flatly refused to have a new main road driven through her property, and so the Ferry Hill site prevailed and work started in 1774. Designed by James Paine and Kenton Couse, the bridge was opened in 1777. A beautiful structure, even after its widening in the 1930s, in a beautiful setting, Richmond must be one of the most frequently painted bridges in England. A decade later Paine replaced in stone the original wood bridge at Kew.

King George III enjoyed Richmond and Kew as a rural retreat where he could indulge his passion for farming. He had a small farm just across the manor boundary in Mortlake, enlarged by the purchase and lease of nearby fields in Richmond, and there – and in the farm lands attached to the old Richmond Lodge – he built up his famous flock of Spanish merino sheep which was regularly auctioned to improve the stock in the country as a whole. He was also a concerned "Lord of the Manor". In enlarging and improving his estates in Richmond and Kew he made a series of deals with the inhabitants, by which old roads across his estate were closed to the public in return for the building or improvement of alternative routes. Some of these deals also included improvements in local government.

The "select vestry", set up in Richmond in 1614, had by the 1740s been replaced by a "general vestry" or general parish meeting. As the latter's powers were undefined, an act of 1766 was passed to establish elected "Parish Trustees". They set about their tasks with a will and considerable success, paving the streets, installing street lighting for the first time, establishing a regular paid night watch with specified beats, and so on. But one of their worries was over the workhouse, first established in 1729. This was now housed in an old rented mansion in Petersham Road, and needed replacement. As early as 1766 the Trustees raised the matter with the King, asking for a grant of land on "Pesthouse Common" – so-called because a pesthouse (or isolation hospital as we would now call it) had been built on the common, outside the wall of the Park, in the late 17th century. The King had immediately agreed, but the Trustees had failed to follow this up as they saw no way to raise sufficient funds to build the new workhouse. It was not until 1785 that a new act was passed, replacing the Trustees by a new elected Vestry with increased powers, and enabling the King and Queen to grant the commons to the new Vestry. The King's benefit from this deal was the closure of "Love Lane" which separated his Richmond and Kew estates.

When the grant of the commons was actually made in 1786, the King himself paid for the building of the new workhouse. The surplus land on Pesthouse Common, some of which was also reserved in due course for a new cemetery, had been granted "for the employment and support of the poor of the parish of Richmond" – and this was the origin of the now very rich Richmond Parish Lands Charity.

The passing of George III marked the end of a royal court in the Richmond-Kew area, though he was by no means the last royal resident. But Richmond had become sufficiently established to survive as a fashionable riverside resort until the coming of the railway provided the third great spur to development.

Richmond had already began to grow in the early 19th century. Much of the new development at that time was a thickening-up of areas in the existing town. But "New Richmond" was developed in the fields along the Lower Mortlake Road in the 1820s with small houses for the artisan and lower working class. Then in the 1840s came new developments in the Upper Field: a row of villas in Friars Stile Road, the development of Park Road, and new large villas on the west side of Queen's Road.

The advent of the railway accelerated this development, as middle class Londoners moved out to enjoy the new country suburb. In the 50 years from 1801 to 1851 the population of Richmond exactly doubled from 4628 to 9255. It had more than doubled again by 1881. The first railway line, from Nine Elms to Richmond, was opened in 1846, with a terminal station on the Kew Road a little south of the present station. Then two years later the line was extended to Waterloo and to Staines and Windsor, and the first railway bridge over the Thames in the London area was built close by Asgill House. A new station for the through line was constructed between the Kew Road and Parkshot. The line to Kingston was opened in 1863; and a line to link with the North London Railway at Gunnersbury and with the City and Hammersmith Railway and the District Railway at Hammersmith followed a few years later, with a new terminal station on Kew Road to the north side of the through tracks.

As an immediate result, the Richmond fields began to disappear under new rows of large and not-so-large villas. The slopes of the Hill quickly filled up, and new development accelerated along the Marshgate

Richmond railway stations c1880. The LSWR through tracks are on the left; the station for these was between Kew Road and Parkshot. On the right is the terminal station for District and North London trains.

*(Photograph in the Richmond Public Library local studies collection, reproduced with permission of the London Borough of Richmond upon Thames)*

Richmond railway bridge when newly opened in 1848, seen from Twickenham Meadows. A lithograph published by Thos. McLean.

(Sheen) Road, the Lower Mortlake Road, and at both ends of Kew Road. (See map on p 42.)

With the opening of Kew Gardens station, the fields on the east of Kew Road were also developed with new roads and houses. Within 25 years of the first coming of the railway, half the fields of Richmond had already been built over. Before the end of the century they had been completely submerged under lines of detached or semi-detached villas or rows of smaller cottages. As the supply of land in the fields dried up, many of the large grounds attached to the big old mansions were redeveloped with roads which still bore the old names: Halford Road, Ellerker Gardens, the Hermitage, Mount Ararat, and so on. By the end of the century, when the population of Richmond already exceeded 25,000, even quite small gardens were being built on, as witness the development of Ormond Avenue in the garden of the Rosary in Ormond Road.

An important development came in the 1890s, when Richmond was the first local authority in the London area to build a "council estate" (in Manor Grove). The so-called "Richmond Experiment" was a great success and was quickly followed by more council house building in the years before the first World War.

For all these new communities new facilities and services were required. New churches were built to relieve the pressure on the parish church. St John the Divine was the first new Anglican church in Richmond, consecrated in 1836. It was followed 20 years later by Sir George Gilbert Scott's St Matthias at the end of Friars Stile Road, then by Holy Trinity, St Luke's and Christ Church. The first new purpose-built Roman Catholic church, St Elizabeth's in the Vineyard, was built in 1824 and was joined seven years later by the Congregational church next door. A Strict Baptist chapel was established in Parkshot in the 1820s, and the main Baptist congregation, after meeting for some years in a lecture hall and then in the "iron church" in Park Lane, brought from Teddington, finally built their curious pyramidal-roofed and bespired church in Duke Street in 1881. The Wesleyans had their own church in Friars Stile Road from 1850 as an offshoot of the great Wesleyan training college built at the top of the hill, just off Queen's Road, in 1843. Ham acquired its own church, St Andrew's, in 1831; while the little chapel of St Anne's on Kew Green, first built in 1714, was enlarged no less than six times before the end of the 19th century.

With the Anglican churches came new parochial schools, and the Noncomformists established the non-denominational "British Schools"

St Matthias (1858)

Wesleyan Chapel, Friars Stile Road (1850)

Duke Street Baptist Church (1881)

The Congregational Church (1831) and St Elizabeth's (1824)

The 'Iron Church', Park Lane (1869)

NEW CHURCHES

at Petersham and then in 1867 in the Vineyard. Richmond was also full of private schools – and most of the large houses in the town became schools at some time or other during the 19th century.

Nor were the more material needs of the new population neglected. Shops spread up Hill Rise and along the bottom end of Kew Road. New small shopping areas developed: in Friars Stile Road, the Sheen Road, the Lower Mortlake Road and around Kew Gardens station. New pubs and alehouses made what in some cases was a quite brief appearance. Some have survived, like the Mitre in St Mary's Grove and the Bricklayer's Arms in the Lower Mortlake Road; but who now remembers the Tam O'Shanter, the Lemon Tree, the Crofton Arms, the Crystal Palace, the Lion and Lamb or the Steam Packet – to quote but a few of the names listed in the 1850s?

The proliferation of pubs and alehouses catered not only for Richmond's increased population but also for the increasing numbers of Londoners making day trips to Richmond by steam train or horse bus. A day on and by the river was the greatest attraction, and Richmond's small community of boat-builders turned into proprietors of great fleets of rowing boats for hire by the hour. Another attraction was Kew Gardens, since 1841 open to the public every afternoon from 1 pm free of charge. (the one penny admittance charge was first levied as a war-time measure in 1916.) Around Kew Green, as in the roads near the bridge at Richmond, tea shops and tea gardens flourished even more thickly than the pubs. At the upper end of this same scale, the Star and Garter provided splendid luncheons and dinners for the gentry who would drive out from London for a day's outing – or just an evening jaunt – in their own coaches.

The Star and Garter had been enlarged again in 1864-65 by the addition of a large residential block in "French chateau" style and of a banqueting hall at either end of the old buildings. When a disastrous fire destroyed the old buildings in 1870, they were replaced by a dining pavilion to seat 250 diners and with 13 additional private dining rooms. Below the Star and Garter another large new hotel was built in 1863-64 – at first called the Richmond Hill, then the Mansion – and now the Petersham. Their chief rival in the town was the Castle in Hill Street, with gardens stretching to the river and with an imposing set of assembly rooms.

The Star and Garter fire in 1870 drew attention not only to the inadequacies of the local fire brigade but also to the failure of the Southwark and Vauxhall Water Company (S and V) to maintain

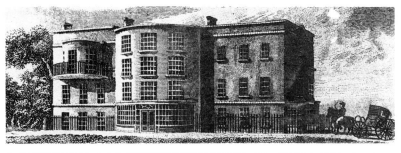

## THE STAR AND GARTER HOTEL

(Top) As rebuilt by Richard Brewer in 1803.

(Centre) Architect's drawing for the reconstruction after the fire of 1870. The new dining pavilion is in the centre. (The towers on the left were never in fact added to the 1865 banqueting hall.)

(Below) 'A Day's Pleasure' – scene in a private dining room as the waiter presents the bill –1842.

Richmond in the 1860s – detail from the six inches to the mile Ordnance Survey map, surveyed in 1863 and published in 1869. Half of the Richmond Upper Field and most of the 'parish lands' on the former Richmond Common had by this date been built over.

*(Reproduced by permission of the Ordnance Survey)*

pressure in the mains. S and V had been supplying Richmond with water since they bought out and closed down the Richmond waterworks in the late 1850s. But the relationship was not a happy one. The water supplied by S and V was of poor quality – and they were charging more and more for it. Eventually the Richmond Vestry decided to set up its own water supply system, from artesian wells. There was a memorable crisis in January 1877 when S and V cut off supplies to the town before Richmond was quite ready, but a series of emergency measures saved the day and Richmond then maintained its own water company until 1965.

The Vestry were now coping with a multitude of problems – public health, sewage, water supply, the maintenance of a proper fire service, etc – that seemed too much for a mere parish authority. There was an increasing public pressure to apply for incorporation as a Borough; and this step was finally taken in 1890. Sir Whittaker Ellis, a son of the one-time proprietor of the Star and Garter and of the Castle, a Member of Parliament and a former Lord Mayor of London, bought up the Castle Hotel (which had been closed for some years) and presented it to the town as a site for new municipal offices. He was elected as the first Mayor of Richmond, and the new Town Hall, with its entrance on the newly-named Whittaker Avenue, was opened in 1893.

Whittaker Ellis had already rendered signal service to the town by helping the Vestry to acquire the hillside grounds of Buccleuch House – to become a public garden as the Terrace Gardens – a few years before. Another major addition to the town's amenities was made in 1898 when the new Council agreed to lease as a recreation ground the 87 acres of the Old Deer Park that were left over when the Mid-Surrey Golf Club had laid out its new course. Already some smaller portions of the Old Deer Park had been leased for the "cricket ground" and the "athletics ground".

The first World War probably made its greatest impact on Richmond by the number of casualties being treated in the several military hospitals set up in the town and in Richmond Park. And it left two lasting memorials – the Royal Star and Garter Home which, after the war was over, replaced the old hotel which had been converted into a hospital for the disabled; and the British Legion poppy factory which took over the former premises of Watney's brewery in the Petersham Road.

The period between the wars saw the development of new housing estates along the road between Petersham and Ham and in the North Sheen area (which had been transferred from Mortlake to Richmond in

1892, when Kew and Petersham also became part of the new Borough[2]).
It also saw the beginning of a process which has continued through the
second half of the 20th century: the destruction of many of the remaining
large old houses and their replacement by massive blocks of flats or,
more recently, offices.

A major change in Richmond's geography was wrought in the 1930s
with the construction of "the Great Chertsey Road", including the
widening of the Lower Mortlake Road, the creation of the Kew Road
round-about and the building of the new Twickenham Bridge. This new
road, while improving Richmond's access to London and to the west,
has also brought greatly increased through traffic, and has done almost
as much as the railway to divide the area by an east-west physical barrier
with few crossing points. If some people now think of anything north
of the A316 as "Kew", it is easy to forgive their misperception.

The second World War, in which Richmond suffered its share of
bombing, interrupted the relentless progress of redevelopment only
temporarily. The most striking changes are to be seen in the big estate
developments at Ham, but the centre of Richmond and the Parish Lands
estate on Queen's Road have also undergone great transformations.
Richmond has been fortunate to escape with minimal high-rise
development; and the recent redevelopment of the riverside from Water
Lane to Bridge Street (though criticized by some who dislike
architectural pastiche) has, in my opinion, much enhanced a vital area
which had become a dilapidated eyesore.

In 1965 the reorganization of local government merged the boroughs
of Richmond, Barnes and Mortlake, and Twickenham into a new
"Greater London Borough of Richmond upon Thames", with its
administrative headquarters in Twickenham. But Richmond has
maintained its identity within the larger unit and – despite the developers
– has kept much of its character. On Kew Green or on Richmond Green,
in the Vineyard or on the crest of Richmond Hill it is not too difficult
to imagine oneself back in the 18th century.

---

2    *Ham became part of the Borough of Richmond in 1933.*

# INDEX

Note: the page numbers of illustrations are shown in bold type.

CW0067126?

# SCARS OF DIVORCE

# ABOUT THE AUTHOR

Michelle Browne was born in Dublin, the second of four children. She now lives in Johnstown, Co. Kildare with her three daughters. Michelle is a highly experienced family mediator, running a busy practice in Naas, Co Kildare. She is passionate about changing how we deal with divorce and separation in Ireland. She works hard with couples to create amicable separation agreements. Michelle wrote this book to start a conversation and to make a change in how we deal with divorce. When she's not busy keeping couples out of court, she's busy taking on a new interior design project and climbing mountains.

Find her at:

www.browneandcomediation.ie
www.instagram.com/browneandcomediation

# Scars of Divorce

How To Avoid Them and Achieve an Amicable
Divorce in Modern Ireland

## Michelle Browne

ORPEN PRESS

Published by
Orpen Press
Upper Floor, Unit B3
Hume Centre, Hume Avenue
Park West Industrial Estate
Dublin 12

email: info@orpenpress.com
www.orpenpress.com

Paperback ISBN 978-1-78605-214-8
ePub ISBN 978-1-78605-215-5

Printed in Dublin by SPRINTprint Ltd

# ACKNOWLEDGEMENTS

Firstly, I would like to thank my parents for their unwavering support throughout the years. For being there, for never judging, for the gardening, for the logs, for cleaning out the fire, for the babysitting. For the love that so many of us born in the seventies in Ireland just know is there without the need for it to be said. I love you both so, so, so much. You have been my cheerleaders, my guides and the most wonderful grandparents any children could ever wish for.

To my two sisters and my brother and my sister-in law, I want to thank you all. I love you all so much.

To my absolutely fabulous girl friends who have been such an integral part of my life over the past decade. Life would have just been dull without you all; may we never stop having fun and adventure.

To my teacher Catherine O'Connell, a very special lady. I want to thank you for your words of encouragement in Maynooth University. It was a privilege to be taught by you. I have never forgotten your kindness. To my classmates in Maynooth University who studied with, laughed, encouraged and supported me and each other through a wonderful journey of learning. To Dr Roisin O'Shea, for all your wisdom and patience thank you so, so much for everything you do. To all my colleagues and friends in IPMO. To my editor, thank you for all your work. To Gerry Kelly for telling me of course I could write a book, thank you.

Finally, to my three beautiful, clever, kind daughters – thank you for just being the best humans ever.

# CONTENTS

Contents

Contents

# Contents

# INTRODUCTION

This is an honest account of heartbreak, healing, and a passionate plea for change. It is a warts-and-all account of a difficult journey through marriage, childbirth, separation, and divorce.

I explain the way we divorce in Ireland (and how we have done so since its legalisation twenty-five years ago) and expose the problems of our court system.

Separation and divorce are traumas, which we have dealt with poorly as a society. We have exacerbated our existing ills and caused all too many new stress-related ailments. How our children fair from our broken marriages – with their protracted court cases and bitter battles – has yet to be fully realised.

There was never a rule book on breaking up and there certainly isn't one on divorce. My generation is probably the first to have taken to the divorce courts en masse. Therefore, our advisers, guiders, and parents are simply not equipped with the knowledge or experience of this subject to guide us, and it certainly doesn't help that the subject is still somewhat taboo. We are hardwired to believe that the justice system will provide the justice we feel is owed to us for our broken hearts and broken homes. Unfortunately, justice for heartbreak is never served in court.

In this book, I address how we, as a modern society, should divorce and separate with the least amount of stress and trauma possible. I break down the pros and cons of each option currently available to couples and clearly explain the processes involved. I outline a step-by-step guide to help those going through this process. I discuss the need to re-examine how we deal with marital breakdown on a societal level, address divorce from a legal perspective, and examine how the government can support each citizen of Ireland in exercising their legal right to obtain a divorce. I share statistics on parental alienation and the findings of a recent international report. I also discuss the pitfalls of parenting through divorce and offer guidance to those enduring this difficult task.

# 1

## THE WHY

### LOVE

Why is love never enough? That feeling of wanting. That feeling of desire. That mad, can't-wait-to-see-you love. The kind of love whose kiss is so hot you don't want to come up for air. That truly, madly, deeply in love feeling of never wanting to be parted. Love that can hold you all evening and it doesn't even matter that their arm is numb. The kind of love that doesn't mind your snoring or care if you've showered. That pang in your stomach. The radiant, unexplainable glow – that flush, that gush of love. We can't help but be ecstatic when it hits us. We are filled with delight when our friends have it too. Love is so celebrated the world over, it even has its own holiday – you know, the one where we spend ridiculous amounts of money on overpriced cards and flowers. Love has a billion and one love songs to sing along to, and when we're feeling it, we sing out loud. So why is it just not enough? Why doesn't it last, why does it go away? Why does it leave scars?

When examining how to divorce well, it is perhaps wise to examine how we love and what gets us to the point where we need a divorce in the first place. Don't get me wrong: I'm not in the business of advice for keeping couples together, though that's not to say I'm advocating for divorce either. People make mistakes and marry the wrong person all the time; that will be part of modern life for evermore. But if we know more about what to look for in our chosen partners and understand what we want for ourselves and our futures, we may make better decisions.

> 'Love is patient and kind; love does not envy or boast; it is not arrogant or rude. It does not insist on its own way; it is not irritable or resentful; it does not rejoice at wrongdoing, but rejoices with the truth.'
>
> 1 Corinthians 13:4-8

Upon reading that very old little verse, my first reaction is that we are slightly misguided as to what love looks like, for the world we live in has changed so much. I don't know why love isn't enough, but it's not. As a romantic, and as someone who can say that I've definitely been in love, unfortunately, I know that love alone is not enough.

I also know that we would benefit from learning a few things about love: the things that can misrepresent as love and the reality of what love isn't. We are then at least informed to make better decisions.

## THE REASONS

Firstly, let's look at the stats: marital breakdown is on the increase – but why? In my profession, where dealing with marriage breakdown is a daily occurrence, this is a question that is put to me regularly. It is something of a curiosity for many and there is a real interest in understanding why some relationships don't work. On the face of it, we know the top reasons cited for marriages not working, which paint a fairly clear picture. However, having personally experienced two marriage breakdowns and having spent hundreds of hours mediating with couples who have decided to call it a day, I can say with certainty that the answer to the 'why' is extremely complex.

Let's address the seemingly less complex top three reasons cited for marriage breakdowns. Yes, there is a pattern, and for statistical purposes, this can be broken down into percentages, so here goes the top three reasons for marital breakdown:

Top of the list is – yes, you guessed correctly – infidelity. Secondly, not far behind, are stress-related issues, which is a very broad spectrum, including alcoholism, drugs, gambling, financial crisis, illness, and the special or extra needs of a child. In third place is the loss of interest in one's partner. Reasons less commonly spoken about, which are less likely to reach the mediation table, include physical and emotional abuse. Like so much in life, just because we don't talk about something doesn't mean it's not happening.

## Infidelity

This is when a person has cheated and a decision is reached to end the relationship. It is indeed a heartbreak; the pain is real and is experienced as a betrayal. It is very sad and can often come as a huge shock, adding to the trauma. Oftentimes when a relationship breaks down due to infidelity, it isn't the first time that the unfaithful partner has betrayed their spouse, which certainly doesn't make the situation any easier.

As for why men and women cheat, the headliners are simpler than we might think: needs not being met, not being attracted to each other anymore, personality disorders, sex addiction, and a lack of emotional connection. On the whole, we believe that cheating is wrong and remorse is usually shown. If we know it's wrong, why do people continue to do it? Do people ever change or is it once a cheat, always a cheat? Haven't we been cheating since God was a boy? Do we now just have less tolerance for bad behaviour or are we being caught out more? Without a doubt, our phones are the number one way of getting caught out. The likelihood is that people have not changed much, but due to changes in technology and our general societal distain for cheating, more cheaters are getting caught out.

More so than previous generations, people of my generation have been taught to value themselves, and this has impacted our decisions to split. The simple fact is that we are legally entitled to divorce, regardless of the reason why.

## Stress-Related Marriage Breakdown

Almost as common as the first reason, the second is what I have referred to as 'stress-related' issues. This is by far the most complex reason, as well as the most wide-ranging. When I first began mediating, I was taken aback by how many marital breakdowns involved children with complex needs. The stress and strain on parents dealing with additional needs and the day-to-day challenges of life is more than anyone should have to face. Fighting for our children to get the education they are entitled to, for extra resources, or dealing with the health system are hard battles for many people, and they can consume parents. Where there are such difficulties, not all relationships survive.

Many relationships have been broken by battles with addictions, wherein hurt people, who are simply worn out by their own battles, cannot see a way forward. Stress breaks down communication and, for many people, it is simply too difficult to go on.

## Losing Interest in Your Partner

Though often cited, this issue is rarely that simple. Decade after decade, we all change in appearance; we all age. So why does some love grow while others lose interest in their partner? Is it just a thing we say when we no longer have the same feelings we used to? Or did we ever have real feelings of love to begin with? Did we just want a family so badly that we decided this person would do, convincing ourselves that we did in fact love them? Did we tell ourselves that it would all be grand, that everyone else was getting married and there was no way *you* were going to be left on the shelf? Or did you not want to upset the parents with coming out as gay? You really liked her and so did the family; did you think, 'I'll get married and we'll all be grand!'? When losing interest, people often lose respect for their partner. A lack of respect in a relationship can be extremely damaging to the self-esteem of the other person.

### VITAL INFORMATION

Having spoken with hundreds of separating couples, I believe we are all capable of talking ourselves into believing what we want to believe. Many of us are chameleons and actors who don't have the true love that we would like others to believe.

Are we really discovering anything new from the top three reasons for marital breakdown? Have we any information to prevent the hurt when this does happen? Will an honest look at why marriages break down help us make better decisions going forward? Will delving into the 'why' have a positive outcome? I have to believe wholeheartedly that the answer is yes. If we can examine what doesn't work and understand the damage caused by picking the wrong partner; if we can have a conversation about the reality of marriage breakdown; if we understand that we have more choices than ever before – more resources, more education, understanding what 'red flags' are – then yes, absolutely. Having an open conversation about 'why' is relevant and necessary.

I should say that sometimes it's not complicated: a person makes a poor decision and, as a consequence, it leads to the end of their marriage. This happens and will continue to happen. However, for a vast number of people, when you dig a little deeper, you'll find there was often a problem with the foundation. The 'why' is the catalyst but the problems are much more complex.

In Ireland, we have a complicated history between church and state to say the least. This has undeniably affected us: Catholic guilt has had a large role to play in our lives. The first divorce in Ireland was granted in 1997.

Figures from the Central Statistics Office show that, in the early 2000s, approximately 5,000 people were recorded as divorced. Roll on to the 2016 census and over 100,000 Irish adults were listed as divorced. In the past number of years, we have seen a steady increase in people applying to our courts for divorce. Data published by the Courts Service shows that 5,856 divorce applications were filed in 2021, representing an increase of 11 per cent on the previous record of 5,220 in 2020. The latest record shows just shy of 6,000 applications in 2022. The majority of cases are dealt with by the Circuit Court system. Why are we as a nation – who only created the legislation for divorce in 1995 – now clamouring to the divorce courts?

Behind closed doors, violence and abuse have occurred within families in Ireland for decades. It was only in January 1991 that rape within marriage became a criminal offence and, in 2019, we passed a law to also make psychological and emotional abuse a criminal offence in Ireland. Though patterns are repeated in life, this is not a necessity. In fact, it is undoubtedly essential that we make a change. Thankfully, change is happening in our world and positive outcomes have been achieved by people speaking out, discussing the issues, and knowing better to do better. However, much more still needs to be done.

A 2005 survey by the National Crime Council and the Economic and Social Research Institute found that 15 per cent of women and 6 per cent of men have experienced severe abuse by a current or former partner in their lifetime. The European Union and the United Nations define gender-based violence (GBV) as 'violence directed against a person because of their gender'. They further state that GBV is rooted in inequality, the abuse of power, and harmful norms, and that while both women and men experience GBV, most survivors of GBV are women and girls. GBV can include sexual, physical, mental and economic harm inflicted in public or in private. It also includes threats of violence, coercion, and manipulation. GBV can take many forms, including domestic violence. While Ireland lacks more recent data on the prevalence of GBV, a 2014 European Union survey examined violence against women (VAW) across EU member states. It reported that, in Ireland, one in four women (26 per cent) has experienced physical and/or sexual violence since the age of 15. When examining statistics on the prevalence of GBV, it is important to keep in mind that GBV is systematically underreported. Underreporting occurs for various reasons, including the cultural acceptability of violence, a nation's level of gender equality, exposure to risk factors for violence, and a nation's overall level of violent crime. As a result, these prevalence statistics likely represent the minimum level of GBV in Ireland.

Statistics from Women's Aid report that one in four women who are in a relationship have been abused by a current or former partner. In 2021, Women's Aid recorded 28,098 disclosures of violence against women and 5,735 disclosures against children.

Men's Aid have reported receiving over 7,561 calls from men in 2021, which is an increase of 37 per cent on the previous year. These calls to their helplines are from men in abusive relationships who need support, as well as men dealing with issues of parental alienation. 94 per cent of this abuse is perpetrated by women.

## RED FLAGS

In recent times, we've heard a lot about being aware of 'red flags' in a relationship. But what are they? To increase awareness, Women's Aid have recently run the 'Too Into You' campaign, in which they list the top ten red flags to look out for:

- They say they *hate your friends* and complain that you spend too much time with them.
- They send you *constant texts* and get mad if you don't reply.
- They *criticise* how you look and tell you how to dress.
- They share or threaten to share *intimate images/videos* of you without your consent.
- They *demand* to *look through your phone* to see who you are talking to.
- They have a *bad temper* and you feel afraid to disagree with them.
- They accuse you of *cheating* on them all the time.
- They threaten to *hurt themselves* if you break up with them.
- They make you feel guilty if you don't spend all your *free time* with them.
- They force you to do things *sexually* that you don't want to do.
- They are *physically violent* or threaten to hurt you or someone else.
- They constantly put you down and *criticise you*.

Other common red flags for abuse are:

- They use your disability to shame or humiliate you.
- They misgender you or use incorrect pronouns.
- They use your fear of the authorities as a way of intimidating you.
- They threaten to 'out' you to your friends, family, or workplace.
- They try to control how much you work, making you depend on them for money.
- They use sign language very close to your face or use threatening gestures and expressions to frighten you.

- They use your children to make you feel guilty, manipulate situations, or threaten to harm or take your children away.

If you don't recognise any of these signs but something feels wrong, it probably is.

## Lovebombing

- Sounds like: 'You are perfect, I've never met anyone as perfect as you.' 'My life would be nothing without you.' 'I want to spoil you.'
- Looks like: Gifts, attention, constant text messages.
- Feels like: You are under pressure to return their feelings. Feeling like you owe them something.

Lovebombing is when your partner 'bombs' you with excessive attention and affection. The honeymoon stage can feel new and exciting, but your partner may use their affection as a way to manipulate and control you later on. This can be dangerous, especially if you feel like you owe them something or can't say no to them after all their attention and affection. This is a form of emotional abuse.
They might say:

- *'I want to be with you all the time; you spend too much time with your friends.'*
  This is a red flag. Your partner should encourage you to spend time with friends and family.
- *'I was so nice to you today, why won't you have sex with me?'*
  This is a red flag. Your partner should not guilt or pressure you into sex.
- *'I like to check on you because I get worried.'*
  This is a red flag. Needing to know where you are and who you are with all the time is very controlling behaviour. This does not show trust in the relationship.

## Gaslighting

- Sounds like: 'You're so emotional.' 'I didn't say that.' 'You're imagining it.' 'I was just joking.'
- Looks like: They deny that things happened. They accuse you of being in the wrong. They make you question everything.
- Feels like: You are going crazy. You are confused, unsure, and insecure. You constantly doubt yourself. You apologise without knowing what you did wrong.

Gaslighting is a form of emotional abuse. It happens when your partner makes you question your own feelings, instincts, and reality. They might say things like, 'You're crazy – that never happened,' 'You're being so dramatic,' and 'You're making yourself feel that way.' They might even play the victim themselves. They do this to make you unsure of yourself so you'll rely more on them.

## Negging

- Sounds like: 'You're actually smart, I wouldn't have guessed it looking at you.' 'You're really pretty for a black girl.' 'Give me three reasons why I should go out with you.'
- Looks like: Banter and flirting. They give you a compliment and insult you at the same time.
- Feels like: You have to prove yourself to them.

Negging is a form of emotional abuse. This is when someone gives you a backhanded compliment or an insult to make you more open to their romantic advances. It is often disguised as slagging, flirting, or banter, making it difficult to know if a line has been crossed. If negging continues over time, you can become desensitised to it, and it can have a huge impact on your self-esteem.

## Available Information

The above information, which is readily available online on the Women's Aid, Men's Aid, and HSE web pages, can help us to recognise emotional abuse and understand that it is a challenge for us all. It can be confusing, which is why it is so vitally important that we have this conversation about what is acceptable and unacceptable in how we treat each other.

Setting standards in a relationship regarding the acceptable behaviour of others will influence what we tolerate in our personal lives. Violence is illegal and unacceptable in our society. We must aim to have the same distain for emotional and psychological abuse towards anyone. The latter is often invisible, but with a collective, cultural, and societal shift, neither we nor our children will tolerate this behaviour.

We need to discuss what we should not accept from others. There cannot be too much conversation about this. Relationships shouldn't be so hard, and the wrong ones can exhaust you and cause psychological and physical harm. Many of us want a fairytale but life is seldom simple. The more we educate ourselves and our children, the more likely it is that we can have healthy relationships and a happy ever after.

If we learn to recognise the signs that our relationships are not working, we can recognise when to call it a day. A little more knowledge brings us one step closer to not marrying the wrong person.

# 2

# A PERSONAL STORY

'The suitcase was empty; I was just teaching you a lesson.'

Only six weeks earlier, I had brought my tiny premature baby home from the hospital. I was in the home I shared with my husband and three girls when he came downstairs with a small suitcase. He said he was leaving, and although I had heard this many times before, the fear of being alone now terrified me. I panicked. I stood in front of the door and begged him not to go, pleaded for him not to leave me. He turned around and walked down the hallway to the kitchen and left through the back door. I followed him but stopped before going outside. With my tiny baby in my arms, I thought I would die. I was physically and emotionally unwell, having had an emergency caesarean section at thirty weeks gestation only a few months earlier. My middle child was fourteen months old and my eldest was ten years of age.

Two days later, my husband returned home. He told me the suitcase was empty and he was teaching me a lesson. I couldn't understand what I was doing so wrong. Why was he so unhappy? I promised to try harder. In my heart and soul, I deeply believed that I was unlovable. My self-esteem was at rock bottom; you could have scraped me off the floor. I couldn't believe I was having to beg this man not to leave me. I truly thought I couldn't cope on my own with my girls, and that if he left I would die. That was, without a doubt, the lowest I have ever felt.

## THE FIRST CUT

I was in my late twenties when my first marriage broke down. I had loved my first husband dearly and he loved me too. We thought we were soulmates. I can't say he was my first boyfriend or I his first girlfriend, but we were still somewhat innocent when we met. I fell with all my heart and so did he. We were well matched, a relaxed couple who did everything together and enjoyed many of the same things. We loved going out or staying in together and we didn't fuss about much. We loved our holidays and enjoyed each other's company. With his comforting arms around me, I loved that he made me feel minded. I trusted him. We were romantic together and loved surprising each other with gifts and romantic gestures. I remember spoiling him with a surprise party with all our friends and family. I truly believed we would be together forever. We shared the same dreams and had big plans for our lives together. When we met, we both had our own homes and were financially comfortable. We had nothing in life to complain about: we were happy. We had a beautiful black-tie wedding. He wore tails and I wore a beautiful white satin wedding dress with hand-beaded embroidery to match a burgundy raw silk cape with a long train. The speeches made everyone cry and we thought we'd live happily ever after. Young and in love, we had never had much to worry about.

When I was six months pregnant with our first child, I woke up one morning with Bell's palsy. It was a terrifying experience but my husband was a great support for me; he always reassured me. I knew I looked like the Elephant Man – my face was shocking; it looked like I'd had a stroke. It was scary and, when I think back, we were babies ourselves. It was our first ordeal to speak of but we got through it together. Ten weeks later, we had a beautiful, healthy little baby girl. He was there through a long and difficult labour, as shocked as I was with our ordeal. We were both delighted to be parents. I was slowly beginning to recover from the Bell's palsy and life was good.

My husband worked hard and we supported each other. We adored our beautiful little girl and planned to expand our family.

One autumn afternoon some eighteen months later, I drove myself to Rathfarnham for a routine pregnancy scan. We were having our second child. I was twenty weeks pregnant and delighted with life. My husband was working and my little girl, who was only one-and-a-half, was with my parents. I didn't mind in the slightest that I was going to my appointment on my own. My husband was a hard worker and I never wanted to pressure him to take time off work. The doctor had delivered my first child so I was very comfortable with him and his wife, the sonographer.

I'll never forget that day for as long as I live. The waiting room had one or two other patients waiting for the doctor, but I was there for the sonographer. I drank lots of water to ensure a full bladder. The sonographer was a slim lady with a mop of blonde hair. She welcomed me into her room and helped me to get comfortable for my scan. She put on the gel, making sure to warn me that it would be a little cold. With the screen pointed towards herself, she proceeded to scan … and scan again. And again.

'Just bear with me for a moment,' she said. 'I'd just like the doctor to check something.'

Lying there waiting for the doctor to come in, I knew there was something dreadfully wrong. I prayed and prayed in blind panic: 'Oh, please, please, *please* God, let my baby be okay!' It dawned on me that I hadn't felt the baby in a while, but I hadn't felt much movement in my first pregnancy, so I hadn't been overly worried this time around. The doctor arrived and he too scanned my tummy. He stopped and put down the scanner. He then gave me the saddest news I thought I'd ever hear: my baby's heart had stopped beating … my baby was dead.

He brought me into his kitchen and sat with me, gave me tea and offered to drive me home or call a taxi for me. He explained that I may begin to bleed and lose the baby naturally, although this may not happen. He wanted me to go home for a week or so. It was explained to me that if nothing happened naturally, I would need to be admitted to the hospital for a procedure. I didn't want him to call my husband; I didn't want to upset him. I didn't want him to call my parents, as I didn't want them to be upset either. However, he did call my husband and I drove to meet him at my parents' house.

As I drove home from Rathfarnham that evening, the life I had planned came crashing down. I worried about how I would tell my pregnant friend, who was due at roughly the same time as me. We had planned our pregnancies so our children could be friends. As we lived beside each other, we had become very close. I didn't want her to worry that this might happen to her.

When I eventually arrived at my parents' house, I put on a brave face and told them not to worry about me, I'd be fine. I just wanted to leave so I didn't have to talk. I couldn't deal with any feelings at all – I didn't want to feel. I took my little girl and quickly left. I immediately went into myself and didn't come out for a long, long time.

Within the next week or so, I was admitted to hospital, where they carried out a procedure to take out my dead baby. I went to the hospital alone and made it difficult for anyone to get close, insisting I was fine. I had carried my dead baby for another ten days before the procedure in Mount Carmel. I continued to see the doctor as an outpatient for a number of months so that he could take bloods and monitor me. He also advised me not to get pregnant again for at least twelve months. Looking back, I believe this also caused me to retreat into myself.

When I look back, I know I didn't share with anyone how sad I felt. I thought I was somehow protecting others by keeping my emotions to myself. I didn't want anyone to feel bad or feel sorry for me, so I toughed it out and went into my shell. It wasn't a conscious decision; it was a reaction. Day to day, I did what I had to do to keep things going, pushing away any real feelings, as they were too hard to bear. I closed off from my husband and, eventually, our marriage broke. Somehow, it didn't survive the loss. I know I pushed him away and I know I was suffering, but I didn't know what else to do. I didn't understand that I was depressed, and I doubt he did either. I remember that a pal of his told him not to put up with me! I can laugh about that now, as we were all so young. I don't blame anyone, but I still feel sad when I recall the person I was then: I can see that she needed help. It was sad and hard to accept.

What happened after the marriage broke down and my husband left isn't something to be laughed at. It's something from which I have learned a lot. There is a saying I believe to be true: 'What doesn't kill you makes you stronger,' and this is eventually what has happened.

Shortly after our marriage broke down, solicitors became involved. I thought I had been in pain for the previous few years but *this* was a whole new level of mental torture. We were pitted against each other in a vicious manner. Very quickly, it became a very nasty battle. Without a clue as to why, I was in a living nightmare – I didn't know *what* was going on! Within a few weeks of solicitors' involvement, communication had completely broken down and we now only spoke through letters sent back and forth by our solicitors.

I have to say, I had a lovely solicitor, the late Andrew Synott. He was a gentleman and he explained the process of separation to me. However, I don't think I understood a word. I do remember that every time I wanted to speak to my husband it was a costly exercise. I remember crying on the phone to Andrew and he was very kind to me. He often didn't know what to say. He worked in a busy practice in Dublin, and had dealt with many difficult family law cases.

Throughout the years of the separation process, there were many, many solicitors' letters sent back and forth – possibly hundreds. We had letters stating times for drop-offs and collections of our daughter, letters with changes of meeting times and places, and letters suggesting bedtimes and the suitability of foods and activities. The state of the relationship between me and my ex-husband was horrendous. Letters were issued by solicitors containing outrageous accusations. Shortly after solicitors became involved, a war was waged that included bank accounts being cut off without any notice. I was at the till in the supermarket when I realised that my bank card wasn't working. My daughter and I had to walk out of the supermarket, leaving behind a trolley full of shopping that I couldn't pay for. My car was repossessed when I didn't even know there was finance on it, and jewellery was removed from my home.

Having never gone through anything like this before, and without any close friends or family with such experience, I just kept going. I didn't know how to change anything that was happening. As solicitors had been employed (and were charging hefty fees), it seemed obvious that we should just let them do their jobs. What happened was very destructive. Since the split, my husband had become a person I just didn't recognise. It never dawned on me that he may have seen things differently, or that we had engaged in a very damaging process. I was incredulous as to his behaviour and the things he had done. I didn't recognise him.

At that time, one of the hardest things to deal with was the bad behaviour of some people in our lives. I don't mean my close friends; I mean neighbours, acquaintances, and some in-laws – grown adults who made judgements when, actually, they didn't know anything that had gone on.

Life was a kind of haze. I was dealing with a marriage breakdown and a young child whilst grieving my sad loss. My only communication with my husband was through solicitors. On top of that, I had people judging me or avoiding me. It's a weird feeling when you know someone is crossing the street to avoid you, or when people look the other way when they used to greet you. People who knew absolutely nothing about my life or my marriage had decided to judge me. My husband lived in a small village and had been there for most of his life. Though I had been there for years, I was still very much considered a 'blow-in'. I think the small-town effect increased the feeling of judgement, as small towns can have the gossip factor. It was very tough on me but I kept my chin up and kept going. I suppose we all have some unconscious biases and judge others sometimes. Whatever the case, it hurt me and it made life even harder, but I just got on with it.

After months of letters from solicitors, spending thousands upon thousands of euros, and shedding many tears, I was given a court date for a legal separation. When I think back to the young woman in that room with solicitors and barristers, I can only feel sorry for her. Phoenix House in Dublin is a busy place. Solicitors and barristers in gowns and wigs are racing around, claiming spots to perch their clients on, and bustling for available private rooms (of which there seemed to be a scarcity). Those clients, who are actual human beings whose lives are shattered, are told to stand in a spot in a cold, bleak room until their representatives return.

Through my solicitor, I had met with three different barristers but I genuinely didn't understand what was going on. On the day of the court hearing, I was crying a lot. I hadn't imagined this for myself and didn't quite know how I had gotten here. I had never had a clear path mapped out in life, but I was someone who, if I loved you, I *really* loved you. I was honest and I cared a lot for the people around me. So how was I here? It was so rotten I couldn't stop crying.

I hadn't brought anyone with me to court. I never wanted anyone to know how difficult it was. I didn't want sympathy – it only made me feel worse. I suppose I put on a front, which is why I don't blame anyone now: no one knew what was going on.

Inside the courtroom, my solicitor put his hand firmly on my forearm.

'Michelle,' he said in a serious voice. 'You have to stop crying. The judge won't give you a separation if he sees you in this state.' He was stern.

Two things happened in the courtroom that day. Number one: the judge asked my husband's barrister a question about access time with our daughter. The barrister looked down at my husband's solicitor for confirmation. They nodded at each other and informed the judge that everything was fine. The judge moved on. I also remember papers being put in front of me to sign. The solicitors had written something in pen on a typed document. When I asked what I was signing, I was told it was just to say that I didn't want any of my husband's pension. That was the first time that a pension had been discussed, and really it wasn't a discussion. It seemed like a mistake that it hadn't previously been mentioned or dealt with. Maybe it was deliberately left until the last second – who knows? I certainly didn't.

The judge granted us a judicial separation. Afterwards, I left the courthouse having said thank you and goodbye to my solicitor and barrister. My ex-husband followed me. I stopped and sat on a wall outside, where he sat beside me and put his arm around me to comfort me. I was still sobbing. I think he was relieved it was all over; he was heading into town to meet a friend. And so life went on.

I have no doubt that his experience was also unpleasant and unfamiliar, but people with different personalities have different ways of dealing with things. I would recover ... but my experience with the divorce courts wasn't over yet!

## Too Much to Bear

I married my second husband in the most beautiful fairytale setting. The sun was shining, the flowers were beautiful, the guests were happy, and a female soprano sang the most romantic song as I walked down the aisle: Roberta Flack's 'The First Time Ever I Saw Your Face'.

It wasn't a long courtship at all. I believed he loved me and that he meant everything he said. I knew we had some problems but I had chosen to believe the words that came out of his mouth. I really wanted to believe them. I already had one failed marriage behind me and, by God, it was easier to believe him than to not be married! Or so I thought. The feelings of failure and disappointment I carried should now have gone away. How wrong I was ... and I was often wrong. I hadn't been a high achiever in school, in sports, or in anything for that matter. Being wrong had become a part of me. Maybe I was set up for a fall; maybe it was just a series of unfortunate events. The only thing I know for sure is that it was cruel. I wouldn't wish on my worst enemy the things I endured over the next stage of my life.

It was like something from a film; a beautiful summer wedding at the Kildare Country Club, one of the finest hotels in the country. Champagne was flowing, the sun was shining, and the guests laughed, enjoying the occasion. Our magnificent suite had a beautiful four-poster bed. Everything was picture perfect.

But from the moment I married my second husband, I couldn't understand what I was doing wrong. I was constantly trying to please him. Nothing seemed to make him happy. I was in a state of rushing, being careful of everything I said, everything I did. It wasn't me, yet it was. How did I get to this point where I was afraid to say how I felt? Why did I always get it so wrong? From the food I cooked to the way I tided, everything I did was making him unhappy.

Shortly after we met, we became involved in business together, so on top of trying to please him at home, I was also trying to please him at work. When I look back, it's hard to find any moments of happiness or contentment. I had begun to believe I was truly unlovable. I was told I had no friends and nobody liked me. It was getting to me. The scraps of attention I received seemed to be for show. The only thing we seemed able to work together on was building the business.

He wanted a family and I wanted my marriage to work more than anything, so I didn't tell anyone what was going on for a long time.

The May before our first child was born, we were on holiday in Spain. It was one of my favourite places to be, La Cala, near Marbella on the Costa del Sol. The trip was for my birthday, which I always enjoyed celebrating, no matter my age. I had become accustomed to my husband being unhappy with me and I had become a people-pleaser, a person I would now like to shake. I knew the more I stayed quiet, the less likely I was to upset him, but this time, he couldn't keep it in. He told me he couldn't stand me and to get out of the apartment and out of his sight. I honestly don't know what I'd done to upset him that time. He stormed out in sheer temper, leaving me in the apartment, but I knew he would be back soon. It was a sickening feeling. I couldn't believe what was happening. No matter what I did, he wasn't happy.

As a birthday gift, my parents had given me a voucher for El Oceano, a nearby hotel and spa, which was only a ten-minute walk away. I decided to pack a bag and leave. I couldn't face dealing with him when he came back.

I checked into El Oceano for the night. Overlooking the sea, it's a modern adults-only hotel with a chill vibe. At the time, there was a girlband staying there, which people seemed excited about. A few staff members had mistaken me for being with the band, which gave me a little lift. I had been feeling awful and I thought this was written all over me, but the band was young and cool so the association was a compliment. Dining alone in the restaurant was very strange, not something I'd ever done before. Was something inside me trying to show me that I could cope alone? I was scared, yet it was relaxing all the same. Just sitting there alone was a big step. I took a deep breath and told myself I was going to be okay. I would be fine.

I was selling a property in Ireland that I had owned prior to meeting my second husband. The proceeds of the sale were to be used to fund the expansion of our business. Suddenly, sitting in the restaurant in Spain, I became worried about that property. It dawned on me that my husband still hadn't put the business in both of our names. Though this was now a big worry for me, apart from that I was okay. *Just breathe, Michelle.* I was trying to convince myself that everything would be okay, yet here I was, alone in a hotel in a foreign country.

My phone never rang. I hadn't returned to the apartment that night. How had he not called to see if I was alive? He was safe in the apartment, while I could have been anywhere, could have been dead! I hadn't gone to the hotel to scare him – he had told me to get the fuck out of his apartment. I asked the hotel if I could use their computer (this was prior to smartphones) and I logged onto the Ryanair website. I managed to get a flight home that day, and I had my passport and a change of clothes with me. Still there was no call from my husband. My friend collected me from the airport in Dublin and, as it was my birthday that night, three of us went out for the evening. It was a strange night and I had a lot to drink. It beggared belief that he still hadn't called.

The next day, we were in my friend's living room. We had all stayed over at her house after our night out. The rest of my family still thought I was in Spain. I hadn't told anyone apart from my two friends that I was home and that my husband still hadn't called. That morning, my friend (who knew that my husband and I had been trying to conceive) looked at me.

'I can see it in your face,' she said. 'You're pregnant!'

She'd always had a sixth sense about these matters. *What the feck!* I had just decided that I'd be fine on my own! *Oh Lord, you can't be serious!*

She went to the shop and returned with two pregnancy tests. Of course, she was right: I was indeed pregnant. While this news percolated with my hangover over the next few hours, I gathered myself and went home. A few days later, my husband returned. Not knowing what to expect, only that I was now carrying our baby, before I knew it I was figuring out how to please and appease him again. The last thing on my mind was being okay on my own – there was no way I could do this alone. Like a flash, I was back to where I had been a week or two earlier.

Life went back to how it had been, but when our daughter was born, things improved for a while. My husband was happy; he adored our little girl. He was there for her birth, which was quick and relatively straightforward. He doted on her and was a good stepdad to my first daughter too. The girls were happy and life was okay for a while. By the next March, I was pregnant with our second child, which was a planned pregnancy. We were under financial pressure and I was dealing with the stress of a recession, alongside seldom getting anything right. Anyone would consider it a difficult marriage. After we split up, people told me that they always felt tension in our home and were reluctant to call in. There was a lot of upset and many rows in our marriage.

On the morning of 10 March 2012, I woke up very early. At thirty weeks pregnant, I had gone to bed upset after yet another row. I went to the bathroom only to discover that I was bleeding. I woke my husband and told him I needed to go to the hospital. He called his brother who lived near us, but there was no answer. He then called his parents, who picked up the phone and were at our house within ten minutes. Both girls were asleep. His mum told me I'd be fine, but I was so frightened I couldn't speak.

When I arrived at the hospital, I was given injections to help with the development of the baby's lungs in case she came early. Nurses tried to reassure me that some bleeding was normal and not to worry, that the baby and I would be fine. My husband told me the same thing but my instinct didn't agree. I was monitored throughout the morning and there was a suggestion that I could go home if I felt okay.

I was going nowhere! I knew without a shadow of a doubt that something was really not right. I felt that my husband just wanted me to be quiet - at this point, I felt he couldn't stand me. I had no support from him whatsoever: he just wanted me to be quiet and not embarrass him. Later that day I was scanned, and it was then discovered that my baby was not developing as she should be. My placenta was badly damaged and the baby wasn't growing, nor was she able to receive the nutrients she needed. My husband became stressed and tried to tell me to listen to the nurses and that I was fine. All I wanted to do was focus on my instinct, which was telling me that if my baby didn't get out soon, she'd have brain damage. I asked my husband to go to Penney's to pick up a toothbrush and a nightdress.

A lovely nurse sat with me while there was a monitor around my belly. She was so kind, trying to distract me with a rugby match on the little TV, all the while keeping a very close eye on another monitor, which showed my baby's heart rate. After a while, she called a wonderful Canadian doctor who came and chatted to me. She told me that my baby was very small but would be better off outside of me. We agreed to do an emergency surgery and, from this point on, things moved very quickly.

I was prepped for surgery and the anaesthesiologist was brought in. I recognised him from the birth of my first daughter, when I'd had a terrible time receiving anaesthetic. However, I didn't have any problems with it this time around. The doctor cut me from one side of my stomach to the other, and although I felt nothing, for some reason I thought my tiny baby was scraped out of me. She was so tiny, the doctor said, 'Oh look at you, you little peanut,' as she held her in the palm of her hand. I remember thinking a 'little peanut' was a cute description in the midst of a hugely traumatic and scary situation. The anaesthesiologist, who was at my head the whole time, lifted my head so that I could see my tiny baby. Her whole body was in the doctor's hand. She was quickly moved to the back of the room, where she was placed into an incubator. My gowned and masked husband was in the room too. He looked shaken.

I was stapled up very quickly, and the pain for the next four days was intense. My baby wasn't with me in the ward, as she was in the neonatal care unit. I had to listen to the other families with their babies and their visitors around them. It was hard to sleep, as I was petrified for my tiny baby, alone in the neonatal care unit. Listening to the other mothers nursing their babies and hearing them cry felt so cruel. I had been through a very traumatic experience: my body wasn't my own and the hospital stay was torture. While I was there, my middle girl took her first steps. No one wanted to tell me in case I was upset about missing out.

My gynaecologist arrived a day or two after the birth of my daughter. I'm not quite sure how I ended up being under her care, but she was not one bit kind to me. She told me I had to leave after five days and could visit my baby in the neonatal unit. I pleaded with her – I certainly didn't want to leave my baby! She told me that if I wanted to stay in hospital, she could have me transferred to St Loman's Psychiatric Hospital. For a long time, I was too embarrassed to tell anyone about that conversation: I was afraid they would think

I was mad. Only three days earlier, I'd had a baby who was ten weeks premature and underdeveloped for her thirty weeks gestation. Her birth weight was only two-and-a-half pounds. I knew that the doctor was a disgrace. If I'd had the energy to make a formal complaint, she might have been taken to task on it, but I had no energy.

The staff in the neonatal unit, however, were reassuring and sensitive about how difficult it all was. I was there every day for five weeks. I would go into a small room (more like a phone box) to attach myself to a milking machine. It was important for my baby's development that I gave her my breastmilk. Since giving birth, I was on this pump like a milking cow a few times a day. My baby was fed with my milk through a tube inserted into her nose, and she thrived. The doctors told me it would be a rollercoaster with lots of ups and downs. It's funny, the way things are explained when no one knows for sure what to expect. But lo and behold, after a gruelling five weeks, we brought our tiny baby home. She was a little doll, and life was indeed like a rollercoaster, only scarier.

Life was difficult. I had lots of help from my parents, siblings, and in-laws, and our neighbours were great, but for much of the time it was me, a double buggy, two small babies, and my beautiful ten-year-old girl. Of course, my little family was precious and I will always be grateful for the privilege of being a mum. Truthfully, however, life was very difficult. When your relationship is broken and you're pretending to everyone (including yourself) that you're fine, it's like carrying a ton weight on your back.

People talk about sleepless nights and describe sleep deprivation as torture. For me, that couldn't be more accurate: I found it very difficult. My tiny baby had taken to holding her breath and turning blue, and this became something I dealt with regularly. I would hold her up in the air and plead with her to breathe, breathe, *breathe ...* and she did. It was absolutely nuts! For almost a full year, I brought a blow-up mattress into her room to sleep (or lie awake all night beside her cot). I was physically and mentally exhausted all the time.

Marriage was harder than ever. My husband was unhappy and I couldn't do anything right. When he returned home after leaving with the empty suitcase, I tried so hard to make him happy. I took him to New York on a surprise holiday for his birthday, which took a lot of scrimping and planning. We moved house and I managed to borrow more money from my parents to get a place that he wanted, where I thought we might be happy. All I wanted was a happy family for my three girls, but he was never happy and made it clear that he didn't want me.

Something came over me when my youngest girl turned two, some kind of inner strength. I told him to go. If he didn't want me anymore, that was fine, just go. He left that night, and it was the last time we were in the same house.

On reflection, I had been living through a nightmare from the moment I married him. I had persevered and tried hard to please him. I did love him. I kept trying to focus on the things that had brought us together in the first place. It felt like I was dealing with a spoilt child: no matter what I did, it wasn't enough. His rhetoric was, 'I'm just not happy.'

By this time, I was a different human being. My heart wasn't broken; my spirit had been crushed. My hope that things could be beautiful, that our family unit could be happy, was gone. Broken. Completely exhausted. But my strength was returning. I still had a lot to learn and much more was going to be thrown at me. Now I knew for sure: what hadn't killed me was going to make me stronger.

# 3

## ... A PERSONAL STORY CONTINUED

So, you think you know a few things about a process you've already been through? Oh, no you don't! I can laugh now. As I regularly tell my mediation clients, your sense of humour will return. Okay, so I do know a few things about the process ... how could I not?

Number one: you won't get a straight answer. The fact is, it's not that simple. There is often no straight answer.

Number two: you'll pay through the nose. This is still the same. It is well known that solicitors charge high fees, with divorcing couples spending anywhere from €20,000 to €30,000 – even €40,000 and €50,000 – on legal fees. This becomes more expensive still when a case is taken to the High Court, where costs can even exceed €100,000.

Number three: you'll wait and wait for a call to be returned and, in all likelihood, it won't be. In my experience, this can especially be the case if you have paid a retainer.

It is understandable why many people in Ireland have a negative view of the legal profession. Of course, this doesn't apply to all solicitors, but my personal experience (along with stories I've heard from many others) unfortunately warrants the bad jokes. It is extremely unfair on clients and is one of the many reasons why change is needed in how we deal with divorce.

For the moment, back to my second divorce. Just when you don't think it's possible for someone to go any lower, they do. This time, I truly believed (and still do) that the system is broken and not fit for purpose – and that's not all: going through a divorce and recognising that you'll have to navigate a broken system is only half the battle. Bad behaviour, greed, nastiness, and personality disorders also have their parts to play. The way I was treated by some legal professionals was as shocking as some of the tales told by my second ex-husband.

At an early stage in the separation process, I was in a meeting at Phoenix House with an accountant, a barrister, and my solicitor. We had hustled for a small room in which there was a bit of a countertop, and we were all standing relatively close together. I was wearing a green coat, which I hadn't taken off. There was a hurried atmosphere – I had only ever felt hurried or distraught in that place. I was as fragile as anyone else would have been in the same circumstances.

It was a complex case, for I had been in business with my husband since before we were married. There was a property, which I under-stood should have been counted as a marital asset. My husband and I had sacrificed through a recession to ensure the mortgage was paid. Although it was partly owned by my in-laws, I was advised that it was a family asset. The barrister was leading the conversation in the room, and I wanted to ask a question about the property. It was not being addressed and I couldn't understand why. I had concerns that it wasn't being included in the case at all. It was as though I was being blindsided so, eventually, I spoke up. I was nervous, feeling outnum-bered and outranked. Though I don't remember my exact words, I asked the barrister a question about what was happening with the property. She banged her fist on the countertop and roared at me, 'Forget about it, your in-laws hate you!' I was utterly gobsmacked and didn't have a clue how to react. I said nothing. My solicitor and accountant looked shocked too, though they were trying not to show it.

After that point, things went from bad to worse with my representation. The solicitor wouldn't answer my calls and, on one occasion, didn't turn up to court. I recall one sitting where the judge was extremely annoyed with my solicitor. He sent a message to him and my case wasn't dealt with at that time. I didn't understand *what* was going on!

During this experience, I witnessed outrageous arrogance from individuals in the legal profession. It seemed that it was easier to bully me into an agreement than to deal with my concerns fairly. To this day, I believe what happened in that room was bullying through and through.

This is only one example of the terrible behaviour exhibited by a legal professional when dealing with my divorce. Unfortunately, I believe there are many more cases like mine. I know there are good and bad people in every profession, and of course not everyone has had the same experience that I have.

I had been dealing with my second ex-husband in a nasty, protracted battle for almost a decade by now. On a spring day in the District Court, at the request of my ex-husband's barrister, the judge ordered a Section 47 report, or child welfare report. I knew this report would be requested in court, as my solicitor had been notified by my ex-husband's solicitor. When my solicitor explained what this report entailed, I was horrified. The idea of my children being interviewed and observed was beyond anything I could have imagined. My three girls were to be watched and reported on, and so was I.

My ex-husband knew I would be distraught. I couldn't hold in my upset for a moment. I told him I was devastated at the thought of our children being reported on, and I pleaded with him not to go ahead with it. Talking to him was like talking to a brick wall. He didn't flinch and had no emotional reaction to my upset. He simply insisted that he was going ahead with it and that he would get as much custody of the girls as he wanted.

I just didn't believe that this was in their best interests. My youngest was still so tiny and I was the one who had primarily looked after her since the day she was born, weighing two-and-a-half pounds. She was an underdeveloped baby, so tiny and delicate. Unless you've minded a premature baby, it's hard to imagine. My ex-husband never liked giving her medicine, and he left her care up to me. I never really minded, as I knew he was nervous with her.

I always questioned his motivation for seeking so much time with the children. I knew him well enough to know it was not about what was best for them. I believed it was for appearances or motivated by finances. At this time, he was running our business (from which he had successfully blocked me) and would never have the time to mind the children himself. It just didn't make sense that this was in the best interests of our very young girls. Regardless, he refused to discuss anything and insisted that I should speak to my solicitor. He was using the solicitor as a reason not to discuss anything with me. It was difficult to manage this situation without becoming absolutely distraught. It was only a short time ago that I was battling to keep our daughter alive, and now the children and I were being put through this process where he could divide them up, in my mind, treating them like commodities. My mind boggled and my heart was broken for them.

Until this point, my ex-husband had been seeing the children every second weekend and one midweek night. He was insistent that he'd take them whenever he wanted to, and he seemed to believe that the Section 47 report would indeed get him whatever he wanted.

From what my solicitor had explained to me, I knew the process of the Section 47 report would be invasive, both for the children and for me. I was told that we would all be interviewed and observed, that the children would be interviewed separately and watched whilst they were playing.

Although I felt extremely uncomfortable with this, I did not agree to his custody demands so I had no choice but to be put through this court-ordered process. The Section 47 report was requested by his barrister and ordered by the judge. I was present in the courtroom and I'll never forget how sick I felt.

Sometime later, I was contacted by the court-appointed child psychologist. She called my mobile and made an appointment to visit me and the children in our home. As agreed, she arrived with her assistant. The psychologist was a pleasant middle-aged lady dressed in black. Her assistant was a younger woman who went off to another room with my children, leaving me in the kitchen with the psychologist. Dressed conservatively, she had a serious demeanour and always remained professional. I offered her tea and she had a glass of water. We sat at my kitchen table, I by the window, looking out onto the garden, and the psychologist opposite me with her notepad and pen. We met twice, speaking for what seemed like hours. She asked questions about my childhood, my parents, my upbringing, and my life. She asked about my relationship with my husband from the beginning, and about my children, our lives, and our routine.

At that time, I felt completely broken. The weight of all that had happened was very heavy. I was struggling and I told her so. I explained to her that life was very hard, that I'd felt very down. I just told the truth – I was so drained I wouldn't have had the energy to lie, even if I'd wanted to. I felt so bad for my children, particularly my eldest girl. She was ten at the time and was very aware that she was being interviewed. Thankfully, the younger two didn't grasp what was going on. They were just drawing and playing with the nice ladies who visited us.

Approximately two weeks passed. It's hard to explain how sick I felt during those weeks. It was a painful anxiety, the kind you feel when you've lost a child in a shopping centre for a split second, but this time it didn't pass after a couple of minutes. It endured in my stomach and in my head. When you're already dealing with a nasty court battle and then awaiting a report to decide on custody arrangements for your children, your head and body feel like a washing machine. It's hard to function but there are no sick notes available, as you don't have an illness. You can't explain to people that this is going on: you're too embarrassed. You're already being judged by the neighbours and gossiped about at the school gates. But somehow, you have to function.

My ex-husband paid €3,000 for the Section 47 report, as he was the one who had requested it. My solicitor called my mobile while I was driving, and I had to pull in.

'It's here,' he said. 'Do you want to come in and read it?'

*No ... yes ... no ...*

'I will, just read it to me please.'

Tears were streaming down my face as I sat in the car. The report was over sixty pages long. It wasn't my property, and the findings were to be given to the court as suggestions for the access order. My solicitor explained that the suggestions should be accepted by both parties, as these reports are usually accepted by the courts and then made into orders. The report said I was an 'exemplary parent'. It suggested that the girls have one night per fortnight with their father, to be increased over time as they get older. It also suggested that their father attend some parenting and nutrition courses. It quoted a lot that he had said about me, including a complaint that I wasn't like my sister-in-law and 'wouldn't stand at the school gates and chat with the other mums'. I was bemused. There were many more quotes like this, as well as more recommendations regarding the children. I was so relieved that it appeared to be fair and honest, genuinely believing it was the best outcome for the children. Although I felt relief, there was no delight in it, as it shouldn't have had to happen in the first place. It was such a very difficult process that could have been avoided.

Again, it was hardest on my eldest child. The irony was that my ex-husband never took her, never wanted her. After eight years as a good stepdad and a consistent part of her life who promised her he'd always be there, he refused to take her. He told me he was advised not to. That was like some kind of added bonus pain for her and I could never wrap my head around it. Then again, I couldn't wrap my head around so much of what had happened.

A short time later, we were back in the District Court, where we were on a list for the access agreement to be dealt with. My mother-in-law sat outside the courtroom reading what appeared to be the Section 47 report. She looked angry. My ex-husband also appeared angry as he paced up and down. Indeed, he was: I felt his wrath following the report on many occasions and for many years to come.

The court order was made in line with the recommendations of the report. My ex-husband was so annoyed. As a very competitive person, this did not sit well with him. He had been spoilt and liked to get his way; he was used to doing whatever he wanted. After the report was released, I could feel his anger as he became more and more vindictive towards me than ever before.

Up to this point, it had been a huge battle to prove my involvement in our business, and it was a battle I felt I was losing. The role I played in the business was being rewritten. Proving the value of a business that had a large cash element was difficult, especially as I had been blocked from the business. Another hurdle was clearly showing how the expansion of the business had been financed. Nothing that my solicitors had told me had transpired.

Once again, we were back at the District Court. At this point, I had a new local solicitor, as things had become very difficult with my solicitor in Dublin, who never seemed to be available. I refused to work with the barrister who had banged her fist on the table in Phoenix House, and another barrister whom my solicitor had employed had been 'silked', meaning she had become a Senior Counsel. I was informed that she would be very busy and may be hard to get a hold of. My former solicitor had tried to encourage me to take my case to the High Court, and I believe he pulled away from my case when I declined.

I had a number of meetings with a barrister who had been 'silked'. She wrote a defence for me which was never used, as I was advised to hire another barrister. I have since learned that she was obliged to continue with my case. I will never forget her words to me in a meeting in the Law Library: 'Family law is like a vegetable soup: you never know what you're going to get.' To this day, I believe this advice should be enough to stop anyone in their tracks from dealing with separation and divorce agreements through the current legal system. I couldn't believe her statement. She added that the decisions made in court can also depend on the humour of the judge – something about his juice in the mornings and how he was getting on with his wife! The mind boggles. This was the big bucks: my solicitor had brought in the most experienced barrister he knew, and this was the best advice available. This was costing big money! On the other hand, the big-buck barristers know the practices of the judges and how they deal with different cases. By all accounts, this is still the way things operate, and I know in my heart and soul that it's deeply wrong.

Back to my case: it was listed again in the District Court. A day out for me now was for my legal separation. The judge listened to an overview of the case and sent us outside to attempt to come to an agreement on the terms of the separation. Along with my recently employed local solicitor, I had a new barrister whom he had recommended. I had met with her once. She was lovely, and she arrived the morning of the court hearing when my solicitor didn't. He told me he was in trouble with the judge and if she saw him, it would only annoy her. I kid you not, that is why he didn't show. Apparently, he didn't have to. This didn't, however, stop him from looking for €30,000 after the separation was granted. That was on top of a retainer *and* on top of the fees I had already paid to my previous solicitor and barristers for their work.

The decisions on the details of the separation agreement were not made in court. They were decided in a negotiation between the barristers in the foyer of the courthouse. This process is often referred to as 'horse trading'. Clearly, the judge who had asked us to go outside and attempt to settle things was to be respected, hence the solicitor not showing his face for fear of annoying her (his words), and the barristers were facing this judge on a regular basis.

This process didn't feel fair or balanced. It was too much pressure – and not just on me. There is clearly pressure on the court system and on the barristers and solicitors. I have no doubt that many people are trying to do what's best, but this isn't it.

When we returned to the courtroom to have the separation ruled, the judge asked if I was okay. I was in an awful state. I couldn't stop crying – yes, again! I was so upset I couldn't speak or catch my breath. I know now that the trauma was just piling up on top of me and I hadn't dealt with it; I had just kept going. I was deeply hurt by how I was being portrayed by my husband's barrister. My legs were like jelly and the tears poured down my face. The judge took some time to ask why I was so upset but all I could get out was, 'It's all so much.' I felt emotionally drained and traumatised – it was equivalent to PTSD.

The judge stated that she didn't want either of us to introduce our children to a third party. I was very pleased with that, though I wasn't sure where it had come from. The judge seemed to realise that the children had been through so much already, and this decision would, in a small way, put a halt to more trauma for them. She also requested that, should either of us have any issues regarding our agreement, we attempt mediation prior to returning to court. I left the courthouse as a legally separated person. A couple of weeks later, my ex-husband moved his new girlfriend in to live with him without any conversation or warning to me or my children.

I was now dealing with an angry ex-spouse who didn't agree with the findings of the Section 47 report. He also had to attend the courses recommended by the court, and this was taken out on me. There was no line drawn and no ability to get on with things – quite the opposite. My dealings with him had never been so difficult. On a number of occasions, he let me know that he and his girlfriend would decide what was best for our children. He now communicated with me on behalf of not only himself, but his girlfriend too. The challenges just kept coming. As they say: 'What doesn't kill you makes you stronger,' and this is still my mantra!

In my mind, solicitor-led divorces have no benefits: the embedded hurt, trauma, and pain for me and my family were plain for all to see. The battle was embittered and prolonged with many, many scars. I truly believe it was badly escalated by solicitors trying to prove their own worth. I saw no signs from the legal teams on either side that they genuinely cared for the welfare of my children or my marriage. No legal representative seemed to had any regard for the welfare of my eldest daughter. The only people who benefit from cases like mine are the legal teams charging excessive fees.

Today, I hold no ill will towards my ex and I genuinely wish him well. I decided to use my experience to make a difference in the world of divorce in Ireland. As time passes, I can accept that the system is broken, and I truly believe that when we know better, we can do better. Though the system is broken, I believe a much better system is in the making. And yes, of course, I still believe that what hasn't killed me has indeed made me stronger.

# 4

# TRADITIONAL DIVORCE

'Akin to using a sledgehammer to crack an egg.'

## THE LEGAL PROFESSION

It takes on average three to four years to obtain a law degree in Ireland, as well as a further three years to train as a barrister. All said, it is at least seven years before you find yourself in the privileged position of representing a client in an Irish courtroom. A law degree requires dedication, academic intelligence, insight, and imagination. The prestigious Law Society of Ireland holds officers of the court accountable to the highest standards. Of course, high standards are what one would expect of those carrying out such important duties. Made up of members of the Bar and the legal profession, the Law Society has its own regulations, guidelines, and disciplinary procedures for members. There are currently no set fees for private clients, as this matter is to be negotiated and agreed between individual clients and legal practitioners. The Law Society requires that there is clarity on fees from the outset. Due to the importance of the legal profession and the law itself, we largely accept that good legal representation is costly.

The family solicitor has predominately been the go-to for separating adults in Ireland. This has been the practice since the inception of divorce in this country in the nineties. Is this the right place for a separating family? Should the court setting, i.e., the opposing counsel, the defence, the claim and counterclaim, the discovery and further discovery, et cetera, be the setup for divorcing couples?

Criminals attend these same courtrooms with the same type of legal representation. The courtroom setting is unnerving and unfamiliar for most people. Separating couples are often dealing with trauma and grief, as the separation of a family is a heartbreaking business, in which big decisions are made in the best interests of the children and adults involved. It is not a criminal offence to divorce, nor should it be. Citizens of Ireland who have not committed a crime should not be made to feel as though they have.

The other significant difficulty with the traditional process is the period between the engagement of your solicitor and your court date. This period can range from months to years, and the reasons for this vary from long court waiting lists, awaiting responses from the other side, a lack of clarity from solicitors, to reasons that are simply unknown. It is an extremely difficult and costly time for the individuals involved, and fees can easily spiral when clients have engaged solicitors.

All married persons in Ireland are legally entitled to a legal separation or divorce from their spouse. This has been our entitlement since divorce was signed into law in 1996. The divorce referendum of 2019 reduced the time required to be living separate lives from four of the previous five years to two of the previous three years.

The Mediation Act 2017 allows couples to legally separate without the need to partake in court proceedings. This legislation also requires that, prior to commencing legal proceedings, solicitors advise their clients as to the availability of mediation and provide information on its benefits, along with the names and contact details of a mediator.

My experience has led me to respond to the above question with a resounding 'no'. Categorically, unequivocally, absolutely: no. A courtroom is not the appropriate venue to deal with sensitive, difficult, and personal family matters, which often involve children. In addition to this, in my professional practice, it has been shown that the legal system further entrenches the positions of the individuals involved in a dispute, causing further damage and destruction. I will endeavour to explain why I believe this so passionately.

Ultimately, the aim of the courts is to create appropriate provision for the children and the parties involved in a case. While this sounds good, in reality, the court process is stressful, contentious, and expensive. It can cause lasting damage that often goes unrepaired.

Judges do not have a magic solution for couples in conflict. They have the power to determine an agreement that they consider fair and in the best interests of the children. In truth, most couples themselves know what is fair and doable for themselves and their families.

It is widely reported that the Irish family courts are under immense pressure. If your court date (which you would have waited months – perhaps years – to receive) is listed to be heard at my local District Court, for example, you will be heard on one of two days in a month. There will be a list of possibly eighty or ninety other couples along with you, all of whom are in similar positions. Your solicitor and barrister are likely to work in this environment on a regular basis. They know that the judge has a long list, and they will be in front of him or her again and again throughout their careers. Is this the best environment for anyone to make life-changing decisions for themselves and their children?

When people are given the correct information, they can make informed decisions. I strongly believe that, unless a person has broken the law, a courtroom is the wrong forum for making decisions following the sad breakdown of a marriage. There is no justice served for heartbreak in family court.

## A Sledgehammer to Crack an Egg

Would you use a sledgehammer to crack an egg? Of course not: it's just too much power, too much unnecessary force. Yes, it will break the egg, it will do the job, and perhaps you could go on to make something with the egg, but it would be ruined with pieces of shell. The shell wouldn't be nice and would upset the outcome. However, had you used the correct utensil, you wouldn't have to deal with the bits of shell. Okay, that might be overstating it – we all know there is a better way to crack an egg. Similarly, for the vast majority of separating couples, court cases are unnecessary.

The traditional route to divorce in Ireland has made life painfully difficult for many people. Stressed, heartbroken, traumatised individuals, who desire only to heal from the heartbreak and grief, to rebuild their lives without their partner, must be given the opportunity to divorce and separate without the added stress of a court case.

For most separating couples, the sledgehammer is the court case, the barristers, the solicitors, and the whole process. It just isn't fit for purpose, and not just because of the long waiting lists and the extremely high costs, although these are two serious problems that people simply shouldn't have to deal with.

Let's address our route to divorce and, as the song says, the rest shall follow. In case you don't know the song, what I mean is, if we examine the manner in which we divorce and choose a more suitable and reasonable route, we then wouldn't have to deal with the high costs or the lengthy waiting lists.

Let's break things down:

## LEGAL ADVICE

As a practising family mediator, it is my legal obligation to make my clients aware that they are entitled to legal advice. It is, however, the client's choice whether they avail of legal advice and, should they do so, it is not mandatory that they engage in serving proceedings on their spouse. In an ideal world, they would simply have a consultation with a solicitor, in which they are informed of the legal process and their entitlements, including the fact that it is not a necessity to engage in proceedings. Legal advice is, of course, only advice, and in my opinion, it is an indication of what to expect, not a guarantee. In my own experience, this advice varies from one practice to another, and this can be very frustrating for clients.

## HORSE TRADING

I first heard the phrase 'horse trading' from a barrister describing the shenanigans between family law solicitors on the steps of courthouses up and down the country. It seemed to me so apt a description, I can't help but use it here. In family law cases, indications as to outcomes are given by solicitors and barristers, whereas the actual outcome should ultimately be determined by the judge. This, however, is all too often not what happens. In many cases, the outcome is determined on the courthouse steps or in the foyer. You can imagine that, with the long lists and the pressure on the court system (as well as on the solicitors and barristers who have to appear again and again in front of the judges), there is very limited time.

I have been that soldier in courthouse foyer battles a number of times, and it appears to me that solicitors and barristers, who regularly appear in front of a judge, really don't want to annoy him or her. In fact, I can categorically say that I have been told as much by a solicitor acting on my behalf. It's no stretch to say this and it makes perfect sense. Therefore, if there is an opportunity for a case to be settled outside the courtroom, solicitors and barristers will try their utmost to do so. This process is referred to as 'horse trading'. I find it difficult to believe that this is best practice for the individuals and families involved in each case. The details of these negotiations – the families, the children, the human cost – appear to be completely lost. Empathy is nowhere to be seen. For me, it is difficult to imagine that fairness is even remotely possible in these circumstances.

## A Legal Obligation

The law stating that solicitors must advise clients that they may avail of mediation is ineffective. In my experience, mediation receives little recognition from many family law solicitors. This is obviously not the case for all solicitors but, from where I'm sitting, it is far too common. Time and time again, I have seen the assertion that mediated agreements are not sufficient if not dealt with by solicitors and barristers. This is not true. Surely the government could put in place a mechanism to increase the effectiveness of this legal obligation so that the law has a greater impact. Perhaps the situation would be improved by a system wherein large financial penalties were imposed upon solicitors who fail to adhere to this legal obligation. There must be a better way forward. Clearly, there is a need for improvement and this could start with enforcing the law. There is just too much at stake here.

## THE ELEPHANT IN THE ROOM

In reality, a sea change in how we divorce in Ireland with a rise in mediation would lead to less work for family law solicitors. Well, I'm just going to say it: this impact on solicitors' pockets is the elephant in the room. If solicitors and barristers were to acknowledge professional mediation as the best route for separating parties, it would inevitably lead to a drastic decrease in their revenue. In discussions around mediation getting the acknowledgement it deserves, this is the big, unspoken elephant in the room.

If the many cases that are suitable for mediation were to cease engaging in legal battles between spouses, if solicitors offered advice without trying to engage clients in court cases, if they advised their clients about mediated agreements and helped them with processing paperwork for consent-based divorces, then we would be left with a minority of divorcing couples needing the full services of solicitors and barristers. I anticipate that this is already starting to happen. Anyone working within family law knows only too well that the majority of cases queuing up for the courts throughout Ireland are suitable for mediation. Let's call a spade a spade; let's call out the elephant in the room. Let's admit it: this cannot be about protecting the revenue of solicitors and barristers. We need to do what is best for our children, our mental health, our wellbeing – *ourselves.*

Don't get me wrong, I can see why established family law practices may be reluctant to change. I understand the pushback. Lately, I have heard a few radio interviews with family law solicitors discussing the legalities involved in divorce with no reference to mediation or their obligation to mention it to clients. A recent article in *The Business Post* had input from a well-known family law solicitor and barrister, who declared that they were best placed to mediate, referring to their knowledge as superior to that of mediators. Clearly, different professions have different skill sets, and when you wish to file a case against another person or when you need a defence, you get yourself a good solicitor and barrister. When you need a separation or a divorce, get yourself a good mediator who practises in that area.

Family law practices are used to the high revenues generated from divorcing couples. They don't want this to change – why would they? Day in, day out, all I hear from clients is that solicitors (not all, but many) pay lip service to their legal requirements to explain mediation to their clients. It's all too clear that, again and again, many solicitors advise their clients against mediation.

There is no question that legal advice is important and I don't question the integrity of individuals working in this area. It is only natural for those practising family law to preserve lucrative practices and conduct their business through the courts. These practices have been in place for many years. It is the process that is wrong and needs to change, as it is not equipped to deal with the needs of separating couples. As part of changing the process, decisions about the futures of families and of children should be made outside of courtrooms, with couples by and large attending court with a consent application. The average cost of a divorce is around €30,000 per party. The key to making better choices is having the correct information.

Divorcing couples are not criminals; they should not have to determine their futures and the futures of their children in a courtroom battle. By nature, court proceedings are acrimonious. A courtroom is not the place for important decisions to be made by stressed individuals.

Ultimately, solicitors and barristers practise in various areas of law, and the area of family law is changing, as it should be. There is nothing personal about family law cases for the legal professionals involved, but it is most definitely personal for the human beings who are divorcing.

## FAMILY COURTS ARE ESSENTIAL

Although many family law cases can be resolved using professional mediation services, it is important to state that many cases do need the legal system to make determinations and enforce court orders. There are cases in which individuals refuse to pay maintenance or withhold access to their children. There are people out there who have no regard whatsoever for the welfare of themselves or their children, and there are people who refuse to do right thing. There are also people who cannot determine for themselves what it fair or right, and mediation services would be unlikely to suit those cases. Couples can become so entrenched in battles that they cannot make decisions in the best interests of their children, thus requiring a judge's determination. In cases like these, court orders are required. I would like to see a system in which complex cases that are unsuitable for mediation are heard by the judge. This is not the case for the majority of divorcing couples. If we change the system so that mediation becomes the default method of separation when it is suitable, this would enable the smaller number of complex cases to be heard by a judge in a timely manner, as court waiting lists would not be clogged up by couples for whom mediation works perfectly well.

## MY EXPERIENCE

When I separated from my husband in the early 2000s, I attended a meeting with my then solicitor and Senior Counsel at the Law Library to discuss my divorce. This is when I was advised that, 'Family law is like vegetable soup.' (*Really? Seriously!?*) 'You never know what you're going to get.' That statement blew my mind. I couldn't understand how this could be. Surely a clear law is in place around family breakup, and a Senior Counsel should be an expert on my entitlements as a separating spouse? This is simply not the case.

## THE HUMAN COST OF OUR BROKEN SYSTEM: A PERSONAL STORY

I recall that in the early days of divorce in Ireland, it was expensive. As a child, I had an aunt who was separated, which was unusual for the time. When I asked her why she never got a divorce, she explained that it was too expensive. I loved my aunt dearly. She worked hard all her life and shared a home with her husband and two children. When her children flew the nest as adults, she also left and moved in with my grandmother. I remember the feeling of injustice; it just didn't seem fair, and of course it wasn't. However, in those days, we were accustomed to unfairness. Courts, legal fees ... these things were so unaffordable, they weren't considered for a second. My aunt continued to work hard and secured a mortgage, purchasing her own home where she could live independently, and she never complained whilst working to repay this. Ten years ago, she died from terminal cancer. Though she didn't have much in the way of monetary luxuries in her life, she was happy; she was a clever, proud, funny woman. I always felt it was unfair that she didn't get a divorce. Even though we as a nation had voted for divorce and enacted the relevant legislation, it simply remained inaccessible for many people.

## WHAT IS NEEDED?

- Recognition that divorce is difficult and the separating parties should be treated with empathy.
- Awareness that the courts system is not the place for dealing with the complexities of a separation.
- A wider understanding of how our courts system works: it is not the answer to dealing with hurt and it does not provide relief for the pain.
- A sea change in the way we divorce. Although the process of divorce is not user-friendly, it is possible for individuals to do it themselves.
- Large legal bills always come with a contested separation or divorce. The most difficult part of divorce in Ireland is not the paperwork, it is reaching agreement on division and provision.
- The law requires appropriate provision for our children, and parents ultimately want the very best for their children. To me, the idea that a long, drawn-out court case is the way to achieve this is absolutely absurd. We must move away from this practice and prioritise the needs and wellbeing of our children.
- A clear understanding of how mediation works for separating and divorcing couples.
- Acknowledgement of the impact upon children when an acrimonious divorce is dealt with through the courts.

Untold damage has been caused over the past two decades. The hurt and destruction to families and friendships is difficult to quantify. Having felt this first hand, as well as having witnessed it daily in my mediation practice, I assure you it's real and the damage is long-lasting.

The traditional legal process typically begins with a legal consultation, followed by the engagement of your solicitor, and then a lengthy process begins with filing your case in the court office. Back and forth applications then result in a court date. More often than not, in reality, cases are settled on the courthouse steps.

There is no evidence to suggest that couples who engage in a courtroom battle are any better off than those who choose the mediation route. There are, of course, obvious benefits to mediation over a courtroom battle. Couples who go through a legal battle are far more likely to find it difficult to coparent, whereas couples who determine their own agreement and have not endured the painful court process will ultimately be less exhausted and traumatised. They save time, money, and their relationships, and they experience a lot less stress.

## MANDATORY MEDIATION

Would mandatory mediation work? Could it help to reduce the numbers waiting on court lists? Would it help with ensuring that couples don't go straight into courtroom battles? Would it reduce stress and parental alienation and improve parenting? Surely if there is a remote possibility of the above, this must be seriously addressed.

The idea of mandatory mediation is not a new one; it has been debated in mediation circles for years. The idea is that mediation would be mandated by law for all separating couples prior to attending court. There are a number of countries in the EU that already mandate mediation for couples with children, and there are other countries that mandate mediation in specific circumstances. I would like to see further support from the government in raising awareness of mediation and its benefits among the general public so that, with the correct information, people are equipped to make the correct choices for themselves.

## PRE-NUPTIAL AGREEMENTS

It is clear that legislation for divorce alone is not enough when it comes to separating couples. Who should be held accountable for ensuring that everyone can access divorce? We now have legislation for legal separations through the Mediation Act, enacted in 2017. This is a very positive, progressive step. However, there is not enough awareness or understanding of mediation. It has been twenty-six years since the first divorce was granted in Ireland, and one would think that the way we divorce in 2023 would be easier. It can be.

Divorce is a part of life and will continue as such for future generations.

I believe that pre-nuptial agreements would assist in dealing with the fallout over finances when a couple splits. On a number of occasions, I have mentioned the possibility of drawing up a pre-nuptial agreement to various solicitors, who simply replied that they wouldn't be worth the paper they were written on. They're just not legally binding, and surely this should be addressed. How much legislation could be required for a contract between two persons prior to entering a marriage? One would imagine this would greatly reduce the number of contentious, financially-driven cases listed for the courts, and perhaps that's exactly why nothing has been done. I'm hardly the first person to suggest it.

## THE CURRENT GOVERNMENT BILL: FAMILY COURTS BILL 2022: SECOND STAGE

My intense feeling about the manner in which people have been dealt with while endeavouring to achieve a divorce or separation in Ireland has been echoed by many and by government ministers over the past number of years.

In February 2023, the Minister for Justice, Deputy Simon Harris, read out the following:

'I am delighted to be here in Seanad Éireann to commence the passage of the Family Courts Bill. This Bill represents a major milestone on the path to achieving the commitment in the programme for Government to enact a Family Courts Bill to create a new dedicated family court within the existing court structure and provide for court procedures that support a less adversarial resolution of disputes.

Reform of family justice and access to a courts system that is less adversarial and reduces the costs of dealing with family issues has long been advocated for. This is not new; it has been sought for many years. It is my aim, as Minister for Justice, and that of the Government and Minister without Portfolio, Deputy McEntee, that a reformed family justice system will enable cases to be dealt with more efficiently and in a way that should ensure better outcomes for families and children.

The measures in the Family Courts Bill will be supported by the first national family justice strategy, which was published in November 2022. The strategy is foundational in nature, recognising the many issues that currently exist with the family justice system and the steps needed to begin its much-needed reform. The Family Courts Bill will provide many of the building blocks essential for this reform.'

The minister went on to say:

'The strategy, which will be implemented over the next three years, has nine goals and more than fifty actions, with the aim of establishing a strong foundation for a future system which is more child- and family-centred, which supports and protects, and which is more streamlined and user friendly.

[...] The Bill provides for the establishment of family court divisions within the existing court structures. There will be a family High Court, a family Circuit Court and a family District Court, each dealing with family law matters as appropriate to its jurisdiction. Each of these family court divisions will have judges assigned to them on a full-time basis.

The Bill provides a set of guiding principles for the family court system to make the best interests of the child a primary consideration in all family law proceedings, to operate in an efficient and user-friendly manner and to encourage active case management by the courts.

A further aim of the Bill is to enable a greater proportion of non-contentious family law matters to be dealt with at District Court level, in order to minimise the costs for litigants and to provide local access to our court system.

A new provision included in the Bill will enable joint applications to be made by spouses or civil partners for judicial separation, divorce or dissolution of civil partnership. At present, one spouse or civil partner must bring proceedings against the other under the adversarial system. The changes should support the use of mediation and alternative dispute resolution in family law proceedings.'

Part Two of the Bill addresses:

'Encouraging and facilitating as far as possible the resolution of issues in dispute by means of alternative resolution methods, such as mediation, except in cases where this would not be appropriate, such as domestic violence cases; promoting and engaging in active case management practices; and conducting proceedings in a manner which is user friendly for the parties, identifies the issues in dispute, minimises conflict between the parties as far as possible, facilitates agreement being reached on the resolution of the issues in dispute, and is expeditious and likely to minimise costs of the proceedings.'

The minister went on to state the importance of the Family Courts Bill in ensuring that:

'Our family law justice system is child focused and child friendly and is reformed to meet the aspirations of Members of this House and the expectations of our citizens, of families at difficult times and, indeed, of our Constitution in ensuring the child's voice is enshrined.'

## PROGRESSIVE IRELAND

Upon reading the above piece, I believe the government accepts that there is a need for change and offers a clear promise that such change will be achieved. However, we still have a system that requires us to wage a war of words with professionals when determining how we raise our children and how we live after a separation. So far, no one has successfully addressed the outrageous fees and the inadequacies of dealing with a marriage breakdown where one party is unwilling to agree to separate. We aren't even scratching the surface of the many problems surrounding divorce in Ireland. Clear guidelines are needed from the government in relation to divorce in Ireland.

## TO SUMMARISE

We understand that divorcing couples should not be punished by a judge for seeking a separation. The priority should always be to organise suitable provision for the children involved.

When communication is just too difficult, we can obtain advice from a third party.

Most of all, we must understand that court battles cause extreme stress and upset to families. Far from alleviating hurt, they create further division and difficulties for years to come.

We need a clear legal system that uses plain English, takes months rather than years, and does not end with 'horse trading' between solicitors and barristers on the steps of our courts.

The current difficulties around divorce and separation in Ireland include the courts system, the long waiting lists, and crippling legal bills for clients, not to mention the difficulties of coparenting after court cases and the negative effects of these things on our mental health. All of this can be avoided through professional mediation.

We need to reform how we deal with divorce as a society. Most importantly, we don't have to wait for the government to make changes to the system: we can inform and educate ourselves in order to make better decisions in the best interests of our families and ourselves. We are acutely aware of the effects of stress on our mental health, and we can effect change by avoiding unnecessary court battles.

Divorce needs to be discussed and the different options highlighted.

We in Ireland live in a seemingly progressive society, where our rights include divorce and same-sex marriage. We care about our neighbours in war-torn countries and we help to house the victims of war. We want to make the planet a better place to live. Although we live in a great country, we can do much better.

# 5

# DIVORCE IN OUR SOCIETY

Divorce is on the increase. It has become part of the world we live in for those of us in Ireland, where we all have a role to play in a functioning, progressive society. When it comes to separation and divorce, there are alternatives to court and they need to become part and parcel of how we deal with marriage breakups.

## HISTORY OF DIVORCE IN IRELAND

The first proposal to remove the prohibition of divorce in Ireland was rejected in a referendum on 26 June 1986. By 63 per cent to 37 per cent, the Irish electorate rejected the proposal initiated by the governing Fine Gael and Labour parties to dilute the constitutional prohibition of legislation that might permit divorce. At the time, the Republic of Ireland remained the only member state of the European Community to fail to make provisions of any kind for the dissolution of marriage.

Holding this referendum reflected the growing concerns within government over the state's failure to deal with the problem of broken marriages. Adopted in 1937, the Irish Constitution reinforced the existing statutory position by declaring that 'no law shall be enacted providing for the grant of a dissolution of marriage'.

In 1995, Ireland held another bitter referendum on divorce. The Irish people were deeply divided, taking to the streets to campaign both for and against the proposal. Pope John Paul II and Mother Teresa both publicly endorsed the 'No' side. The influence of the Catholic Church on voters was seen as crucial for the 'No' side, with Catholic bishops declaring on national television that voters needed to examine their consciences, warning that divorce was 'un-Catholic' and would lead to instability in Irish society. The Catholic Church put a lot of pressure on its members.

Led by John Bruton, the Fine Gael-Labour-Democratic Left government of the day proposed a new amendment to allow for divorce. The government pushed back against the 'No' campaign, insisting that it was a democratic right of the citizens of Ireland to be able to divorce. The Taoiseach viewed it as imperative that Ireland amend the Constitution to allow divorce, worried that another 'No' vote would damage the nation's image as a tolerant and progressive country. He encouraged people to vote 'Yes' in a number of radio and television interviews. He passionately addressed the Irish people, asking:

> 'Is it the Ireland we like to present to the world, as a place that has very strong beliefs but doesn't need to enforce them by law, that welcomes people with a different point of view and treats them well? Or an Ireland that's so afraid, it has to use the criminal and civil law to enforce a particular set of beliefs?'

On 24 November 1995, 62.15 per cent of Ireland's registered voters turned out to cast their ballots and approved the Fifteenth Amendment of the Irish Constitution by a margin of slightly more than 0.5 per cent. It was an extremely close call with Ireland voting for divorce by 50.3 per cent. The amendment was signed into law on 16 June 1996. This referendum only legalised divorce in cases where couples had been separated for at least four of the previous five years. Proponents of the separation of church and state hailed it as a victory to be built upon. On 30 November 2019, the law on divorce in Ireland was changed, reducing the waiting time from four of the previous five years to two of the previous three years.

Represented by Minister for Justice Charlie Flanagan, the government announced that they wished to 'ease the burden on people whose marriages have broken down'. The Minister went on to state:

> 'The Bill will reduce the emotional and financial distress experienced by couples whose marriages have sadly broken down. This legislation will ensure that the process for obtaining a divorce is fair, dignified, and humane. While core protections for marriage continue to remain in our Constitution, this Bill allows both parties to move forward with their lives within a reasonable timeframe.'

The Thirty-eighth Amendment of the Constitution (Dissolution of Marriage) Act 2019 was signed into law on 11 June 2019. The Act provided for the following amendments to the Constitution that were approved by the people in a referendum on 24 May:

- Removing from Article 41.3.2 of the Constitution the minimum living apart period for spouses seeking a divorce.
- Replacing the text of Article 41.3.3 on foreign divorces.

The Thirty-eighth Amendment of the Constitution (Dissolution of Marriage) Act 2019 did not change the other provisions in the Article 41.3.2, namely that:

- Only a court many grant a divorce.
- Divorce may only be granted in cases where there is no reasonable prospect of a reconciliation between the spouses.
- Proper provision exists or will be made for the spouses, any children of either or both of them, and any other person prescribed by law.

Additionally, the Bill provided:

- Applications for judicial separation can be made after one year of living apart, whether or not the respondent spouse consents to the decree of judicial separation being granted.

- A reduction in the minimum living apart period for divorce applications from four of the previous five years to two of the previous
  three years.
- Clarification of the meaning of the 'living apart' requirement for
  judicial separation and divorce applications by giving certainty
  to the interpretation that has been given by the Irish courts to
  that requirement. The Bill provides that spouses who live in the
  same dwelling as one another shall be considered as living apart
  from one another if the court is satisfied that, while so living in
  the same dwelling, the spouses do not live together as a couple
  in an intimate and committed relationship.

## CATHOLIC IRELAND

Catholic Ireland is alive and well. This phrase came to mind recently
when a client of mine asked me to change my payment link that
was issued to him for a mediation appointment. The payment link
showed up on his bank account, and he was extremely upset that
the bank might realise he was attending mediation for separating
couples. After a discussion with my client, I have made changes to
ensure that no payment links will show 'Mediation Services' in the
description on the bank statement or anywhere else. I am acutely
aware of many clients who are extremely affected by the thought
of their neighbours knowing about their marriage breakdown. The
notion that Ireland has progressed past 'Catholic guilt' is unfortunately not the case for everyone. The fact is, we are a predominantly
Catholic country, and guilt surrounding marriage breakdown has kept
many couples in unhappy marriages for years.

## WHAT IS SOCIETAL CHANGE?

In essence, the definition of 'societal impact' or 'social change' means
any significant or positive changes that solve or at least address social
injustice and challenges. Both the public and private sector can push
for changes that have a wider societal impact. Since the beginning
of time, human beings have changed and adapted the ways in which
we live.

In today's world, the changes we see in society take many forms and address issues such as climate change, human rights, and cultural norms. Our collaborative efforts as a society have the ability to generate great change. It is important that we recognise how powerful we can be. This is part of what makes our progressive little nation great. Much of the progress made has been pushed for and led by great organisations such as Focus Ireland, Safe Ireland, LGBT Ireland, and many more.

## CHANGE IS POSSIBLE

Many societal practices went unchanged until we knew better. For decades, men and women were persecuted by the laws of the land. It was only in 1993 that homosexuality was decriminalised in Ireland, and in 1973 the ban was lifted on the employment of married women in the civil service and wider public and semi-state sectors. We voted in favour of divorce twenty-five years ago, and today we recognise that we have a legal right to obtain a divorce. As a nation, we appear to have come a long way on many important issues.

Or have we? Why are so many families devastated by divorce and crippled with guilt – and if not crippled with guilt, crippled finan- cially? Why is it so difficult to obtain a divorce in Ireland, and why do you only have to open a Sunday paper to read about the cost of divorce and the broken courts system? Why have we been unable to address this issue and make divorce accessible for all?

Unfortunately, Catholic guilt has a massive negative impact on the lives of many people in Ireland in 2023. How do we even begin to deal with Catholic guilt? What does it look like and how can we make a change? In addition to Catholic guilt, we have our good old human nature causing us to pass judgement on other people and their situa- tions. If we knew the torturous effect of judgement and understood what bias and unconscious bias look like, perhaps we would think about how we treat others. The vast majority of people are good and mean well for others. A simple, commonsense approach is as good as any to be taken here. When we know better, we can do better.

The way we approach the issues that impact all of us in society has a bearing on how we cope, thrive, or regress as individuals on our personal journeys. This goes for our friends, our loved ones, our families, and ourselves. On our journeys, we have children, jobs, lives, and purposes. Both as a society and as individuals, we can impact our own lives and the lives of others by addressing how we judge, how we act and react, and how we support each other.

The root cause of divorce is conflict. Whatever preceded this conflict is another issue altogether. All of us face conflicts, differences, and pain in our lives, and we encounter difficulties with others throughout our day-to-day activities. How we deal with these difficulties directly impacts our health, wellbeing, and happiness. Currently, conflict resolution and other related subjects are not commonly featured in school curriculums. Perhaps our ability to deal with conflict is genetic, or perhaps it is cultivated by our upbringing. It is most likely a combination of the two. If we understand ourselves and our reactions to conflict, we are a step closer to understanding and accepting conflict as a part of life.

There are a few different questionnaires you can find online to help you to understand your own personal conflict style, which you may find useful. Learning about conflict and acknowledging that we can improve our standards of living by addressing this are key to effecting change. This leads me directly to the technical difficulties of obtaining a divorce in Ireland.

We have been technically divorcing with the services of solicitors and barristers for over two decades, choosing them as our allies in battle. This has been the way we divorce and, to a large extent, still is. I wholeheartedly believe that we have got this badly wrong. We go to our solicitor with the belief that a battle is needed to achieve fairness or to deal with the conflict that has resulted in our separation. Ultimately, we make legal cases against each other in divorce, and the mechanism for traditional divorce in Ireland is therefore combative and destructive.

I also want to address how difficult it is to technically divorce and how we, as a society, can improve this horrendous ordeal. How can we make it less difficult to achieve a divorce? And how can we change societal judgements and improve the way we react to divorcees?

Do we, as a society, believe that the more something costs, the better it must be? I strongly believe many of us do. However, this is

simply not the case when it comes to divorce and it is far too important to let this go. It is completely unnecessary that we pay such high
legal fees to achieve a divorce, when this is something to which we
have a legal right. It is not good enough that we have had to deal with
this unnecessary part of the divorce process for the past twenty-five
years. We must stop accepting this practice.

When it comes to separation and divorce, the Irish people have
been subject to unnecessary fees and an unnecessary system. We
have been pitted against each other in battles where the only surety
is a bill. The law states that we are entitled to a divorce and that
correct provision must be given to the parties and their children. This
law has allowed for far too much interpretation by the legal profession and, when examined, it is clear there is a better way.

For a moment, imagine the following scenario: both parties to a
divorce seek legal advice from two different family law solicitors,
whose practices are across the road from each other in any town in
Ireland. Both parties declare that they want a divorce and ask their
solicitors the same questions as to what should happen. They take
notes of the advice and recommendations based on the full disclosure
of their means. They then swap solicitors and ask the same questions. (Pretend for a moment that the solicitors don't know they are
married.) They then compare their notes. All being equal, with the
solicitors acting in line with the law, the parties should have received
similar advice, made similar notes, and would clearly see the futility
of a court battle.

Obviously, this scenario does not take into consideration that
divorcing couples are usually engaged in conflict. They are most likely
upset and perhaps dealing with some form of grief. Therefore, the
responsibility of dealing with divorce must lie with us as a society,
and we should understand that divorcing couples have not committed
a crime and do not need to engage in battle.

If solicitors advise based on the law and their experiences of the
field in which they are practising, both parties in the above scenario
should receive similar advice. When we think about it in this way,
regardless of a married couple's assets and liabilities, solicitors are
practising the same law. It does not vary from town to town or county
to county. Divorcing adults are not criminals, nor should there be a

need to build a case or a defence. There is a need to examine the parties' assets and liabilities and what is in the best interests of the children involved.

The alternatives to court battles need to be laid out bare. How many practices went unchanged in society until we knew better? For decades, men were paid more than women for the same work, married women weren't allowed to work, and gay people were unable to marry. Courtroom battles between spouses who are not criminals must become a bygone practice.

## DIVORCE IS ON THE INCREASE

In 2020, One Family reportedly experienced an increase of 20 per cent in the demand for their services for lone-parent and separating families. There was also a 17 per cent increase in the demand for courses on parenting during a separation. A press release stated:

> 'Ireland is facing a tsunami of separations and divorces following the pandemic, and family law and support services are not prepared, according to One Family - Ireland's national organisation for people parenting alone, sharing parenting, and separating.'

Many people working in the area of family law and related services have reported the same increase in marriage breakdowns. There is a wide consensus that the pandemic and lockdowns acted as catalysts, exacerbating difficulties and increasing conflict. Increasing numbers of people have applied to the Circuit and High Courts for divorce in recent years.

Reports in newspapers and in the media confirm the issues we face surrounding divorce in Ireland. Guidelines on divorce are available online. On the whole, we accept that divorce can be achieved, albeit through massive ordeals in the courts.

This aside, Irish society has come a long way from the divided nation that fiercely campaigned and marched in the streets to protest legalising the right to divorce. To think that only twenty-seven years ago, half the country believed we should not be able to leave a marriage, regardless of the circumstances! For today's generation, it is inconceivable that such rights were so blatantly non-existent. As a society, we have come a long way in those twenty-seven years.

It is both unfortunate and tragic that, despite our progress in recognising and legislating for the right to live our separate lives through divorce, we have simply not provided a fair pathway to achieve this. However, as discussed in the previous chapter, the government has recognised the many problems in this area and has developed a strategy to reform the family law system. Subjected to traumatic and costly ordeals that are extremely stressful and damaging, we as citizens have been struggling for over two decades to achieve our legal right to divorce. The only people who have benefitted from divorce are the solicitors and barristers turning a profit. The legislation of divorce brought with it a new market for the profession of family law solicitors specialising in separation and divorce. The family law system is grossly unfair and largely inaccessible for many people, and this practice of attending two separate solicitors and waging war on our spouses after a sad marriage breakdown must end.

I know and accept that the government will make amendments to these procedures, and things may improve for divorcing couples as a result. As a society, we can also create impact through how we choose to deal with our own divorces.

## THE POWER OF SOCIETY

When it comes to divorce and society, progress has thankfully been made through changes in the law. The problems around obtaining a divorce are clear, and the alternatives are in place and legislated for (the Mediation Act, 2017). The next step is a sea change in how we treat each other during a divorce. For me, this is a necessary societal change that we can achieve as a nation.

We no longer find it socially acceptable to drink and drive or slap our children, and these things are not tolerated from a legal standpoint. While some people unfortunately continue to drink and drive, it is certainly not treated with approval in our society. Indeed, many of us are only a generation away from a mammy who ran after us with the wooden spoon, and if we were caught, we felt it! Thankfully, most children today would be utterly shocked if a wooden spoon was used for anything but stirring cake mixture. These examples of societal changes were led by amendments to the law, which carried through to our personal behaviour. In my experience, the practice of taking your spouse to court is traumatic and harmful, and needs to become a practice of previous generations. If we disapprove of the physical trauma caused by slapping a child, the same should surely apply to the unnecessary mental stress and trauma inflicted on children by a court case.

The mechanism for avoiding court battles during a divorce is, in fact, already in place. In our society, we have choices and can make a powerful change. When we know something is wrong, we must stop ignoring it. We need to support each other as best we can when dealing with difficult situations. Divorce is a part of our lives and we must choose the best way to deal with this, both for our children and ourselves.

## WHAT HAS NOT BEEN SAID?

The government can do more to help: better guidelines should be published stating what correct provision looks like, what marital assets are, and what rate of maintenance should be paid. Clarifying this would take care of much of the backlog and would deter many courtroom battles. Government guidelines on these matters should be published to raise awareness, and the language should not be over-legalised, as this creates a situation where only solicitors and barristers can profit from this knowledge.

Recently, a government campaign (using taxpayers' money) high-lighted and raised awareness of the menopause and its symptoms, information which is all available through a quick Google search. Surely we would be better served by a campaign highlighting a pathway for people to access their right to divorce and mapping out the most effective way to get there. The negative impact divorce has on people – including children – is well documented, so surely the government has a responsibility to address this.

Furthermore, legislation could very easily be put in place to do the following: prevent individuals from dragging their spouse through the courts when they have not committed a crime; consider mandated mediation for couples with children; and impose financial sanctions on solicitors who do not adhere to the law currently in place around mediation. Far too many people suffer when they cannot access divorce, and a government campaign is needed to explain that divorce is everyone's legal right. Throughout Ireland, many men and women are in unhappy relationships and, for complex reasons, believe they cannot leave. It is commonplace that one party to a marriage will not agree to a separation or divorce, and the other party therefore believes they cannot get out. Though society has progressed so much in many areas, more must be done to normalise divorce. More can and should be done to make the breakup of a marriage acceptable, free from blame and judgement. More must be done to create the kind of system and society where divorce can be obtained if and when required, as is our legal right.

# 6

# MEDIATION

## An Introduction

If you've read a newspaper or listened to the news recently, you'll no doubt hear that a mediator has been involved in a negotiation, or that a judge has directed a case for mediation. As a profession that is respected across the world, mediation is a universally recognised tool for dealing with wide-ranging disputes. It is seen as the most progressive way to deal with conflict and is becoming common practice. It is also, in my opinion, the best way to deal with separation, divorce, and parenting agreements.

The definition of mediation may vary slightly from one organisation to the next. However, mediation is a confidential, facilitative, and voluntary process in which we attempt to deal with disputes to reach a mutually acceptable agreement with the use of a neutral third party. A mediator can take a number of approaches, the most common being evaluative, transformative, and facilitative mediation. There is much to be learned from understanding these different methods but, in my experience, people simply want to know what mediation can do for them.

The Mediation Act 2017, which recognised mediation in law, has made significant changes in how we can choose to deal with separation and divorce by setting out the enforceability of mediation settlements. The Act allows for the parties to a separation to determine if and when a mediation settlement has been reached and whether this is to be enforceable between them.

Change is long overdue in how we have dealt with divorce in Ireland since its inception almost twenty-five years ago. Our courts system is not the right place for people who are hurt, distraught, and broken hearted. For far too long, we have been paying through the nose for something to which we have a legal right. It is not necessary to conduct our divorces through the courts, as we have been doing. When we know better, we can do better – that is my belief and why this information is so important.

But why? Let's examine exactly why we are being led down this very expensive, very destructive, and often very lengthy path. I suppose many of us will just do what the practice has been for years. Perhaps another main reason is fear. Also, many of us share the idea that we are protected by the law, so we go to a solicitor who practices law. For all the above reasons, we have been listed for courts throughout the country and embroiled in conflicts with our spouses. The current family law system is not fit for purpose. This opinion is held by many legal professionals and I agree wholeheartedly. However, the importance of obtaining legal advice cannot be overstated when engaging in a legal issue. Does this sound like mixed messages? Indeed it does.

We can attend mediation in order to come to a mutual agreement between the parties without the need to attend court. That is as clear a description of mediation as one can give. Unfortunately, there are a lot of mixed messages out there about mediation, and it's unfair that the public cannot more readily access the information they need.

Having said this, mediation as a standalone profession in Ireland is still a relatively new concept. The idea that you call a mediator when you're in need of a resolution to a dispute still has a way to go. However, things are changing rapidly, and I firmly believe that mediation will become the go-to for the vast majority of people dealing with separation and divorce in Ireland.

There is much to be learned from understanding the different methods and styles of mediation, as well as from academic writings and the insights of experts in the field. However, it is my experience that people simply want to know what mediation can do for them and how it works. I will do my best to explain as clearly as possible what mediation is all about and why I personally advocate for it. I will then share with you the teachings of some of my favourite renowned mediators.

## WHAT IS MEDIATION?

In essence, mediation is a process of resolving disputes facilitated by an independent third party. The third party – your mediator – is outside of the dispute. It is a confidential and voluntary process in which we attempt to deal with disputes to reach a mutually acceptable agreement. Your mediator should use a number of resolution techniques and creative problem-solving methods, all whilst processing emotion, listening, and using empathy. The mediator's ability to listen and unpack the issues is key to the success of the mediation.

To assist with the process, the mediator may offer their own opinion. Mediation is about listening to a story, acknowledging, and reflecting. It is about framing the issues, identifying problems, asking powerful questions, using empathy, and getting beyond someone's position to move to their interests. It is about underlying what people's interests are, not their positions. Your mediator is unbiased: they are not a judge. Professional mediators do not take a side; they are of no use if they do so.

## Confidentiality

Everything in mediation, including oral statements and notes, is kept confidential. Trust between the parties and their mediator is essential to the success of mediation. A confidentially agreement is signed, meaning that, from the outset, the parties understand that an agreement is in place. This can be built upon to create trust between the mediator and their clients. However, this does not protect a client's disclosure of crimes or threats to themselves or another party.

## Voluntary

The current position on mediation in Ireland is that parties attend on a voluntary basis. Of late, there has been much debate on this subject. Should this status change? If so, what would the implications be? For me, there are pros and cons to both voluntary and compulsory mediation. The very nature of voluntary attendance means that parties are partaking in negotiations of their own free will. This should, in theory, add to the effectiveness of the outcome. The opposite of this, of course, is a court-ordered settlement.

Should there be a process in place for compulsory mediation? This would create the opportunity for parties who would otherwise be facing a court battle to enter mediation, enabling them to reap the benefits of a negotiated settlement and avoid a court case. There is most definitely a case to be made for compulsory mediation.

## Impartiality

A mediator's position is that of a neutral third party. There has been many a debate on whether you can truly be neutral, whether neutrality means you don't have an opinion, and the ability to effectively mediate a positive outcome. Personally, I consider myself to be multi-partial, meaning I am committed to everyone's best interests and reaching the best outcome for all.

I have had clients who were initially worried about the fairness of mediation if there was a perceived wrong on either party's side. A mediator simply cannot to do an effective job if they take sides. In my role as a mediator, I reassure parties early in the process that I will not judge and that I am on neither party's side. Most of the time, parties understand this and appreciate the fact that there is no judgement whatsoever in the mediation process. They therefore feel reassured throughout the process.

### A CASE STUDY: SEPARATED HUSBAND AND WIFE

### Context:

*The couple have been living apart for over two years. Both parties had engaged solicitors to act on their behalf to issue separation proceedings. They had sent a number of solicitors' letters back and forth to each other. There was little or no communication between the parties. The breakup of the marriage followed the long mental health battle of Party A, for which she was* diagnosed and treated. She had removed her husband as next-of-kin in her medical documents and instated her brother. Prior to the breakdown of the relationship, both parties had enjoyed a close relationship with each other's immediate families. There are two children of the marriage: a boy (9) and a girl (12).

Party A contacted me by phone after her counsellor recommended she speak to me. Party A wanted to know what could be achieved through mediation. Her main concern was that she did not want to be in a room with her spouse. I explained to her the process of mediation and informed her that she did not have to mediate with her spouse in the room if she did not feel comfortable. I told her that, upon signing an agreement to mediate, I would be happy to discuss further details with her. (I regularly ask clients not to give me too much personal information over the phone: there is always a tendency for clients to divulge personal information prior to signing a contract.) After a discussion about the process, Party A asked me to contact Party B and establish if he would partake in mediation.

I telephoned Party B and left a message. It wasn't long before he got back to me. With a sense of relief that communication may recommence, Party B was keen to get the mediation process started. I contacted Party A to let her know that Party B was keen to achieve an agreement through mediation.

Prior to their meetings, which were booked in for the following week, I emailed both parties an agreement to mediate.

## Outline:

The first intake meeting was with Party A in the meeting room at my office. The meeting took just over an hour. Party A described her mental breakdown, her recovery, and the fact that she believed she had the capacity to determine what was best for herself and her children. Because the nature of these discussions is more often than not extremely upsetting for the clients, I try to limit meetings to approximately one hour.

The meeting with Party B took place the same week, also in my office. Party B was open about his desire to have an *amicable agreement made in the best interests of the children. He believed Party A to be the best person to predominately raise their children.*

*My objective in the intake meeting is to get as much of an understanding of both parties as possible in order to:*

- *Understand what has brought them to this point*
- *Find out what worked well for them prior to the breakdown of the relationship*
- *Determine what is important to them to achieve now*
- *Determine any common areas of agreement*

*For clients who are reluctant to tell me what has gone on, I use an analogy of a messy press to explain that, sometimes, in order to sort the mess inside, we need to empty the press out first. We can then put things back in such a way that we can get what we need.*

*In this case, Party A was comfortable in explaining to me what had happened in her marriage to this point. She described a lot of hurt and pain and she had exact dates that were of importance to her. These were the dates of incidents of conflict, as well as dates that signified meaning in relation to her marriage and how she felt Party B saw the relationship. Party A had a fixed position on the division of assets. She also greatly desired being able to coparent.*

*It was very important that Party A felt listened to and heard. She was engaged in the process and was happy to be listened to.*

*That same week, Party B attended his intake session of mediation alone. He was also happy to be in a position where he could be listened to. He held the position that he did not want to continue with legal proceedings. He believed that there was no value to the court case, which would inevitably happen if they did not attend mediation. Although Party B was more matter-of-fact about their relationship breakdown, he too explained that their marriage had been a difficult journey over that past number of years. He explained that he had a lot of previous experience of legal cases and did not want to proceed down a legal route with Party A.*

*Both parties expressed to me that they felt mentally exhausted from the difficulty journey they had been on.*

*With both parties, I reflected upon how they felt and what was important to them. The common ground was the children. Early into the mediation process, I asked both parents to fill out a parenting questionnaire. The voice of the child was brought into the mediation room whilst speaking to both Party A and Party B. I asked both parties what they thought the children would want, should they be in the room. The parents took their time to consider the children's needs. It was very apparent that they were on the same page about how they wanted to raise their children. A parenting agreement was written with both parties wanting very similar styles of parenting. I scheduled times for activities with mum and dad and I included arrangements for holidays and Christmas, drop-off and collection arrangements, how best the parties would communicate, and what communication for the children would look like. We included details on education and which schools the children would attend, which was extremely important to both parties. The parties were happy to be able to see a future in which they could parent together.*

*Party A has told me that she can now see a future and is relieved that mediation was recommend to her.*

*Party B told me that, for the first time in two years, Party A came out of the house and said hello when the children were leaving with him.*

*Up to this point, the process of mediation was carried out in individual meetings, which did create an extra onus on me as the mediator to ensure that there was clear self-determination by the parties throughout the process. This elongated the process, as I needed to be very careful in conveying this to the parties, which I did through dialogue.*

*Shortly after the parenting plan was implemented, the parties agreed to come in for a joint mediation session. I carried out a pre-planning assessment by gathering the parties'* statements of needs and the financial documentation they had previously provided.

In the first joint session, I reflected on the progress made so far, in that the work put in by both parties had successfully created a working parenting plan.

At this point, there were a number of outstanding issues to be resolved between the parties. I used the 'pin model' to establish the areas of importance to them. I framed their needs and reflected to them the issues they each considered important. From discussions with the parties, I identified options for development. Using a flip chart, I created a visual of what their options would look like.

There was an impasse on a specific area regarding the division of assets. Identifying why the parties were stuck took some time and I sat in silence for a period. I asked the parties to explain which parts of the options would work for them and which parts would be difficult. This brought to the forefront that there was mistrust around finances. Creating a solution that worked for both parties came from a compromise involving the division of company shares. Settling an agreement around an unknown area allowed the parties to come to their agreement.

During mediation, the question was raised about what they wanted their futures to look like. Both parties had the opportunity to acknowledge where they saw themselves and their roles. Neither of them wanted to take from the other anything they had prior to the breakdown of the marriage. This revelation was made following questions that were posed about how they saw each other's futures.

I drew up an agreement and both parties agreed to attend the office to go through it and sign together. Both parties have agreed to return to mediation should they have any difficulties with their parenting plan in the future.

The key to this agreement was listening to and understanding what was going on for both parties, then asking questions that allowed them to understand how the other was feeling. Finding a common ground early on played a large part in the successful outcome of the mediation. The parties expressed the hurt that *they felt but it was not enflamed. Therefore, everything that had gone on became manageable; they could put it behind them and see a plan for the future.*

*During the course of this mediation, I spoke in my learning and sharing group and to my mentor about determination and capacity. Although my client had suffered with mental illness, I was confident that she had the capacity required to mediate.*

## WHY CHOOSE MEDIATION?

By choosing to partake in mediation, we choose to create our own agreement. We are choosing to listen to the opinion of the other side as part of this process. We are aware that we cannot resolve the dispute without professional help, and we have decided to listen and look for the opportunity to have our story heard. We recognise the need to be treated with empathy, and rather than seeking a victory, we are partaking in a method to resolve conflict.

Mediation offers participants the opportunity to re-establish a connection on a new footing and a different path. Mediation can shift conflict, anger, and hurt towards reconciliation and restoration.

Conflict is a part of life. It has happened since the beginning of time and will continue until the end. Discovering a better way to deal with disputes is part of the process of finding a better way of life.

## Mediation Allows Space

The mediation process allows parties to reflect on their own situation and, with the assistance of a skilled mediator, see each other's positions. This allows for the space that is required in conflict to address important issues, which is key to resolving the issues in dispute. The mediation process allows for the agreements to be reality tested. The skilled mediator will deal with what the future of the agreement looks like.

In addition to academic knowledge, working with people requires the ability to understand them. It is important to give people the time and space they need when dealing with conflict, and mediation affords them this opportunity. Dealing with the different perspectives of individuals and understanding that people may never see things the same way is also a key skill for mediators. Allowing people the space to see that the other party views the situation differently is very important. Through mediation, the parties can acknowledge that we can live with seeing things differently and move on. It allows for the opportunity to apologise without fear of repercussions.

We achieve this by using the skills held only by seasoned mediators. In my own mediation practice, I regularly use the analogy of the messy press. We simply cannot sort it out without taking out the contents and looking at what we can do with it. Though we want to define paths for ourselves and our children, we are often in a place where things feel like a mess. When things are broken down into bitesize, manageable pieces, this process can help parties to see where they are going and what they want that to look like.

## Future Relationships

The process of mediation is designed to create a fair agreement. For separation and divorce, the full and clear disclosures of assets and debts are essential. The importance of this is set out in the Mediation Act and is ensured by your mediator. The importance of creating and ensuring fairness for both parties in their negotiated agreement is clear and cannot be overstated. When there are children involved, ongoing and effective communication is imperative for the future relationship. The manner in which we separate or divorce is key to the success or failure of this future relationship. Parenting is part and parcel of your mediated separation, with the parties sharing parenting responsibilities.

## WHAT MEDIATION IS NOT

Mediation is not counselling or therapy. Your mediator is not allowed to practise law or therapy in mediation, but the process may have a therapeutic effect and the mediator may reflect on legal matters. Mediation allows for the continuation of relationships after the agreement has been reached. To assist in reaching an agreement, the mediator may discuss your BATNA (Best Alternative to a Negotiated

Agreement) and your WATNA (Worst Alternative to a Negotiated Agreement).

## THE MEDIATION ACT

In 2017 in Ireland, we brought in the Mediation Act, which states its purpose as follows:

> '[...] to facilitate the settlement of disputes by mediation, to specify the principles applicable to mediation, to specify arrangements for mediation as an alternative to the institution of civil proceedings or to the continuation of civil proceedings that have been instituted; to provide for the codes of practice to which mediators may subscribe; to provide for the recognition of a body as the Mediation Council of Ireland for the purposes of this Act and to require that Council to make reports to the Minister for Justice and Equality as regards mediation in the State; to provide, by means of a scheme, an opportunity for parties to family law proceedings or proceedings under section 67A(3) or 117 of the Succession Act 1965 to attend mediation information sessions; to amend the Guardianship of Infants Act 1964, the Judicial Separation and Family Law Reform Act 1989 and the Family Law (Divorce) Act 1996; and to provide for related matters.'

This Act is hugely significant in dealing with separation and divorce, stating that a binding legal separation can be reached through mediation. The Act has changed and will continue to change how we can choose to deal with our legal separations and divorces. I have listed sections of the Act which I feel are important and I will explain why:

1. The section of the Act entitled 'Enforceability of mediation settlements' states: 'A mediation settlement shall have effect as a contract between the parties to the settlement except where it is expressly stated to have no legal force until it is incorporated into a formal legal agreement or contract to be signed by the parties.'

2. The Act states that there must be an agreement to mediate, which must be signed by the parties and the mediator. It must also include the terms of the mediation, the time and place that it is to occur, the fees and costs, and the manner in which they should be paid. It should note that the mediation is to be conducted in a confidential manner, as well the right of each party to seek legal advice.

3. The Act refers to the duty of the mediator to determine whether they may have any actual or potential conflict of interest. If so, he or she may not mediate for the individuals involved in this specific case.

4. It is also outlined that a mediator should furnish the parties with a copy of any code of practice he or she may have.

5. The Act also states that the mediator shall act with impartiality and integrity and treat the parties fairly.

6. The Act outlines that the mediator will 'complete the mediation as expeditiously as practicable having regard to the nature of the dispute and the need for the parties to have sufficient time to consider the issues, and ensure that the parties are aware of their rights to each obtain independent advice (including legal advice) prior to signing any mediation settlement.'

7. The Act also states: 'The mediator may, at the request of all the parties, make proposals to resolve the dispute, but it shall be for the parties to determine whether to accept such proposals.'

8. Part Three of the Act is entitled: 'Obligations of Practising Solicitors and Barristers as regards Mediation.' This section states:

   ▪ *'A practising solicitor shall, prior to issuing proceedings on behalf of a client –*
     (a) *advise the client to consider mediation as a means of attempting to resolve the dispute the subject of the proposed proceedings,*
     (b) *provide the client with information in respect of mediation services, including the names and addresses of persons who provide mediation services,*
     (c) *provide the client with information about –*
       (i) *the advantages of resolving the dispute otherwise than by way of the proposed proceedings, and*

(ii)  *the benefits of mediation.'*

The above points from the Act are important for anyone considering beginning or about to begin the process of forming a separation agreement. The points I have covered show the obligations of your mediator prior to commencing any mediation, which are similar to the obligations of any family law solicitor dealing with a separation or divorce. The points set out in this Act are not optional: they are the law by which all mediators and solicitors should abide.

## WHAT MAKES A GOOD MEDIATOR?

Professional mediators have acquired the necessary skills and knowledge to act as ethical mediators, including an understanding of the different conflict theories, conflict dynamics, and conflict management processes. They learn the different conflict styles and develop awareness of their own preferred styles. Among other skills, mediators learn negotiation theory, skills, and practice, all of which are part of their academic learning. This forms the basis of the mandatory standard for mediators.

## Mediation Experts

What makes for a skilled, standout mediator? What makes mediation work?

In the industry, there are many committed professional mediators, none more so than Kofi Annan, Jon Myres, Geoff Sharp, Bill Marsh, and Ken Cloke, all of whom are recognised professionals within the industry, who have garnered much success and raised the profile of mediation across the world.

Ken Cloke is a highly acclaimed, world-recognised professional mediator, dialogue facilitator, conflict resolution systems teacher, public speaker, and author of many books about mediation. In his book, *Mediating Dangerously*, he challenges the mediator to mediate on the edge, encouraging them to delve into danger with asking dangerous questions:

- What have you done to create the very thing you are most troubled by?
- What have you been clinging to or holding onto that it is now time for you to release?
- What are you responsible for in your conflict that you have not yet acknowledged to the other person? What is it they or you did that you are still unwilling to forgive?

I could read Ken Cloke all day long – his wealth of experience is outstanding.

Another highly accomplished mediator is Michael Lang, author of *The Making of a Mediator*. He explains mediation as artistry:

'You are taking the discussion, focused on the overarching issues as well as the moment-to-moment exchange of perspectives. You have a heightened awareness of your own place in the process and are mindful of the parties, the issues, and their interactions. Your attention is so intense that you are unaware of time passing. The conversation and your interventions are effortless, yet measured and purposeful. There is a sense of progress, without an effort to make something happen. You are engaged, pulled into the tasks of the mediation, but the work seems effortless and graceful. The process is elegant, flowing, and productive. This is the experience of artistry in mediation practice.'

These experts, along with many others in the field, prove without a shadow of a doubt that mediation is indeed a highly skilled profession.

## WHAT MEDIATION MEANS TO ME

For me, successful mediation is built on trust. Without trust, it would be impossible for a person to hand over their sadness and concerns to a mediator to assist them in creating a plan for themselves and their loved ones. Successful mediation is centred on people and their ability to feel comfortable in a uncomfortable situation. It is about the connection, the feeling, and the setting. Empathy and understanding are essential components of creating the right environment. As a mediator working with divorcing couples, I know that people can be at different stages of grief or acceptance regarding these issues, and we must be prepared for that. For the mediator, there is a curiosity to delve beneath the surface to understand what more is going on. The energy that the mediator brings into the room is vital, and each client must be able to work at their own pace, which in itself is a task to be mastered. It is also important to have my toolkit to hand (virtual toolkit, that is). The mediator's tools include: the ability to reframe issues, to identify clients' BATNA (Best Alternative to a Negotiated Agreement) and WATNA (Worst Alternative to a Negotiated Agreement), the ability to paraphrase, to actively listen, and to acknowledge feelings. If the opportunity arises, an apology can be a powerful tool. For me, moving towards a resolution will happen much more smoothly when the hurt can be addressed. However, it can also happen without this, and agreements should be made wherever possible.

## MEDIATION FOR SEPARATION AND DIVORCE

From practice to practice, you may find different variations of the same process, as mediators may have their own protocols. In my view, however, the clarity of the processes involved in mediation are exactly why this route is by far the best option for separating and divorcing couples.

The Mediation Act 2017, which recognised mediation in law, has made significant changes in how we can choose to deal with separation and divorce. As well as setting out the enforceability of mediation settlements, the Act allows the parties to a separation to determine if and when a mediation settlement has been reached between them. The parties are also able to decide whether this mediation settlement is to be enforceable.

This means we can attend mediation and come to a mutually binding agreement without the need to attend court. This description of mediation is as clear as any. Unfortunately, there are many mixed messages out there about mediation and it's unfair that the public cannot more readily access the information it needs.

Further discussion and examination on the divorce process in Ireland and the cost of same will only serve to improve the process for those who will need it.

**Fear:** The fear that we will be subject to an unfair agreement or process if we are not represented by a solicitor.

**Protection:** We often believe that our assets will be best protected if we go down a legal route with a solicitor.

**Hurt:** When we are hurting, we often believe we cannot deal with a process that involves the person who has inflicted the hurt upon us.

**Revenge:** The desire to hurt the person who has hurt us leads us to a battle ground. The emotion that comes with hurt and betrayal and sometimes humiliation can fuel the feelings of revenge. However the reality of acting out a revenge as seen in television dramas are best left there. The compelling sense that satisfaction will be achieved with revenge does not have a bearing on the reality of divorce. Revenge is not dealt with in divorce courts or mediations. The Hollywood movies depicting justice being served for wrongdoing are fantasies.

## What Can Prevent Mediation from Working?

Fixed or preconceived ideas can prevent us from trying something new. It is very easy to believe an assertion we have heard. We may believe that mediation won't work for us because we've heard that 'John' and 'Lisa' have spent ages in mediation and it was a waste of time, they ended up in court anyway. Mediation isn't a religion; it doesn't require faith for it to work. Mediation is a proven, workable process with many benefits and few (if any) downsides.

Mediation will work at the parties' own pace. However, it can be prevented from working if a person enters into it without having accepted responsibility for their actions. Parties who are finding the circumstances of their breakup extremely difficult may simply be unprepared to engage in the process. In such a situation, it is difficult to proceed towards a successful agreement. In cases like these, some counselling can also help.

The Mediation Act states that your solicitor must not only advise you to try mediation prior to commencing a legal case, they must also make you aware of the benefits of mediation and provide you with information on the process. Despite the Act's clarity on the legal position on mediation, it unfortunately appears that the Act is rather ineffective in this regard. I am personally aware of many clients who have come to my practice without having received any such direction or information. All too often, clients take legal action against each other, becoming embroiled in a battle which is extremely difficult to come back from.

Additionally, clients may choose to take the advice of legal professionals and then find that they don't want to see the process through. This choice is obviously personal for every individual.

## My Top Tips for Effective Mediation

- Don't object to the other side choosing the mediator; this shows goodwill and cooperation from the other side.
- Get a clear understanding of the process before you start.
- Have a pre-mediation session with your mediator to be sure you are ready to start the process.
- Be concise; don't assume the other party knows what you're thinking.
- The devil is in the detail: when it comes to your agreement, small things really do matter. Be sure to think ahead.
- Leave your conflict in the mediation session. Try not to let it continue when the session is over.
- Try to respect the process you have signed up for. Remember why you're there.
- A good mediator will help the parties to articulate their positions. Even when the parties disagree, understanding the perspective of the other side is vital.
- Work with a mediator who is experienced in their field of practice.

# 7

# PARENTING

## An Introduction

The love we feel for our children is unlike anything else. Though hard to describe, it is an immense, unconditional, deeply protective feeling and a source of joy and happiness. Over the years, this love for our children has been captured in the lyrics of many famous songs and works of literature. It evokes a sense of boundless comfort and bliss. The first steps and first words of a child fill a parent with indescribable excitement and pure pride. With ambitions, hopes, and dreams for our children, a parent's love is unmatched. None of this can be disputed.

However, in reality, parenting is difficult. For some of us, it can be extremely challenging and draining, both emotionally and physically. Parenting is a complex job, which often comes without reprieve or appreciation. A parent may experience their child's path as a rollercoaster of highs and lows. As parents, we feel our children's pain and wrestle with decisions to always do what's best for them: neither to give them so much that we spoil them, nor to let them miss out; to teach them right from wrong; to teach them kindness, but not make them so soft that they get hurt; to teach them independence, but also let them know we're there for them no matter what; to teach them the value of money, but not worry them with the price of commodities; to ensure they always feel our unconditional love.

There is no rule book for parents. We act instinctively with learnt behaviours from our own upbringings, as well as the insights we have received from others. We naturally want better for our children than the opportunities and education that were available to us. We happily make sacrifices for those cherished humans we call our children.

Why is it that, despite this love for our children, there are so many court applications concerning them listed for courts throughout the country? This is happening in vast numbers. How do so many of us end up here? The answer is complex, the damage unquantifiable. Judges throughout Ireland, who often have limited time and long lists to get through, are tasked with making decisions about the welfare of our children. These decisions are frequently made following receipt of a file, which cannot possibly show the full picture. This can happen after a long day of cases being heard before yours is reached. There is very little data available in Ireland regarding the impact of divorce on children, the number of expert reports carried out by court-appointed psychologists, or the effects (if any) they have on our children. We know little about the number of barring or protection orders made in Ireland during separations and divorces. Neither do we know how these cases were resolved or how many of these orders were dropped before the cases were completed. People are vulnerable when dealing with these matters in the courts. They are dealing with the most difficult situations imaginable, which simply wouldn't be on your radar unless you work in the area or have similar personal experience.

Although we are statically unclear as to the details of the families going through the courts system, it is safe to say that many are experiencing highly acrimonious breakups. As a result, they are navigating the broken family court system in Ireland.

As discussed in an earlier chapter, the government has a strategy and has promised to improve the family court system. This is a positive development, headed in the right direction. However, it is simply not enough: too many children are suffering. As parents, we can and must do better.

## CHILDREN'S RIGHTS

Children's rights are a major consideration in mediation. Mediators ensure that the voice of the child, including their needs and interests, is central to the discussion. This is also the case in Irish courts. When it signed up to the United Nations Convention on the Rights of the Child in 1992, Ireland committed to promoting children's rights. These rights include the right to healthcare, education, and to be treated equally. This Convention has 54 articles, which I have listed below. Many of them state the obvious but, unfortunately, these rights can be overlooked when parents are going through an acrimonious breakup. As adults, we all have responsibilities, both in our professions and our parenting, to be mindful of children's human rights.

Article 1: Everyone under the age of 18 has these rights.

Article 2: All children have these rights, no matter who they are, where they live, what their parents do, what language they speak, what their religion is, whether they are a boy or a girl, what their culture is, whether they have a disability, or whether they are rich or poor. No child should be treated unfairly on any basis.

Article 3: All adults should act in the best interests of children. When adults make decisions, they should think about how their decisions will affect children.

Article 4: The government has a responsibility to make sure children's rights are protected. It must help families to protect their children's rights and create an environment where children can grow and reach their potential.

Article 5: Families are responsible for helping children to learn to exercise their rights and ensuring that their children's rights are protected.

Article 6: Every child has the right to be alive.

Article 7: Children have the right to a name, which should be officially recognised by the government. Children have the right to a nationality (to belong to a country).

Article 8: Children have the right to an identity – an official record of who they are.

Article 9: Children have the right to live with their parent(s) unless it is bad for them. They have the right to live with a family who cares for them.

Article 10: If children reside in a different country to their parents, they have the right to be together in the same place.

Article 11: Children have the right to be protected from kidnapping.

Article 12: Children have the right to give their opinion and for adults to listen and take it seriously.

Article 13: Children have the right to find things out and share what they think with others by talking, drawing, writing, or in any other way unless it harms other people.

Article 14: Children have the right to choose their own religion and beliefs. Parents should help their children to decide what is right and wrong and what is best for them.

Article 15: Children have the right to choose their own friends and join or set up groups, as long as they aren't harmful to others.

Article 16: Children have the right to privacy.

Article 17: Children have the right to access information that is important to their wellbeing from radio, newspapers, books, computers, and other sources. Adults should make sure that the information children access is not harmful and should help children to find and understand the information they need.

Article 18: Children have the right to be raised by their parents, if possible.

Article 19: Children have the right to be protected from being hurt and mistreated in body or mind.

Article 20: Children who are adopted or in foster care have the right to care and protection.

Article 21: Children who cannot be looked after in their own country can be adopted in another country if this is what's best for them.

Article 22: Child refugees have the right to special protection and help, as well as all the other rights in the Convention.

Article 23: Children with disabilities have the right to special education and care, as well as all the other rights in the Convention, so that they can live a full life.

Article 24: Children have the right to the best healthcare possible, safe water to drink, nutritious food, a clean and safe environment, and information to help them stay well.

Article 25: Children who live in care or in other situations away from home have the right to have these living arrangements looked at regularly to see if they are the most appropriate provisions possible.

Article 26: Children who are poor or in need have the right to help from the government.

Article 27: Children have the right to food, clothing, a safe place to live, and to have their basic needs met. They should not be disadvantaged so that they can't do many of the same things as other children.

Article 28: Children have the right to a good quality education. They should be encouraged to attend school to the highest possible level.

Article 29: Education should help children to use and develop their talents and abilities. It should also help them learn to live peacefully, protect the environment, and respect other people.

Article 30: Children have the right to practise their own culture, language, and religion, or any of these things that they so choose. Minority and indigenous groups need special protection of this right.

Article 31: Children have the right to play and rest.

Article 32: Children have the right to protection from work that harms them and is bad for their health and education. If children work, they have the right to be safe and paid fairly.

Article 33: Children have the right to protection from harmful drugs and from the drug trade.

Article 34: Children have the right to be free from sexual abuse.

Article 35: Children have the right to be protected from being kidnapped, bought, or sold.

Article 36: Children have the right to protection from any kind of exploitation.

Article 37: Children have the right to protection from punishments that are cruel or harmful.

Article 38: Children have the right to protection and freedom from war. Children under 15 cannot be forced to join the army or take part in war.

Article 39: Children have the right to receive help if they have been hurt, neglected, or badly treated.

Article 40: Children have the right to legal help and fair treatment in the justice system, which should respect children's rights.

Article 41: If a child resides in a country where the laws provide better protection of children's rights than the articles in the Convention, those laws should apply.

Article 42: Children have the right to know their rights. Adults should know about these rights and help children to learn about them too.

Articles 43 to 54: These articles explain how governments and international organisations like UNICEF will work to ensure that children and their rights are protected.

If you have read the above articles, you'll likely expect that all of the above rights are in place for every child in Ireland. Shockingly

- and with great sadness for me, as a mother of three who has endured two divorces and works full-time with separating parents - it is all too frequent that basic rights are not afforded to children due to difficulties surrounding separation and divorce. This is not to say that any parent intends to take away the basic rights of their children. However, the fact remains that, if we do not make extensive changes to how we deal with divorce, we will continue to negatively impact our children.

## PARENTAL ALIENATION

As a professional family mediator, it is important for me to be aware of parental alienation, what it is, and what it means for the children at its centre. Parental alienation can be either intentional or unintentional. Unfortunately, is it very common in acrimonious divorces. The government's Justice Plan 2023 and Family Justice Strategy 2022-2025 both commit to addressing parental alienation. To enhance understanding of this complex issue, in 2021 the Department of Justice commissioned research in this area, which was carried out by experts and resulted in a 159-page report. The findings were centred on: parental alienation in both the European and wider jurisdictions; the nature, definition, characteristics, and relevance of parental alienation; and a comparison of how parental alienation is dealt with across jurisdictions. With regard to parental alienation in an Irish context, the report stated the following key points:

- Different authors have defined the concept of parental alienation differently, although each identifies the rejection of a parent by the child and the role of the other parent in this. Differentiation has been made between parental alienation and parental estrangement.
- No attempt has been made to measure the prevalence of parental alienation in Ireland. Neither has any attempt been made to identify the sociodemographic characteristics with which it is associated.
- There is a lack of consensus in understandings of parental alienation in Irish court cases, highlighting the complexities of

assessment, the use of expert evidence, and issues around the child's right to be heard.

- As has happened elsewhere, some cases in which parental alienation claims are made are high-conflict, protracted cases.
- Interventions include orders for therapy for parents and children, directions to parents to promote good relationships, and considerations relating to transfers of custody.

Further information is included in this report, which provides a huge insight into this area and the workings of the Courts Service of Ireland. The full report can be found online at www.gov.ie.

## WHAT REPORTS MEAN FOR PARENTS

As a mediator, I have seen many family law reports and related statistics. At times, it has been my instinct that these findings and statistics aren't doing much to help those struggling with separation, divorce, and parenting. Knowledge is key to improving anything, and the more we learn, the more we can improve. It can be helpful to discover how other countries with better outcomes deal with the issues we are facing.

The complex issue of parental alienation is appearing with increasing frequency in difficult separation cases. I fear that this is becoming a term that is bandied about in courtrooms without any clear verification by (or on behalf of) parents who are entrenched in legal battles, while their advisors build cases and pit the parties against each other.

I consider parental alienation real, understand its importance, and realise how it can happen. In many cases, I believe it can indeed happen unintentionally. However, I don't want it to be used as another weapon in battle.

## REALITY TESTING

When parents are entrenched in legal battles, they must face the reality that their children may be caught in the crossfire. Therefore, engaging solicitors to take cases against our spouses should be the last port of call, avoided wherever possible. It is our responsibility to exhaust all other options before engaging in battle. Whether or not parental alienation is taking place, our children must be protected as much as possible from hurt and stress.

One would imagine that, for an objective person who is not entrenched in a legal battle, the best process for dealing with decisions surrounding children after divorce is a no-brainer. One of the options involves courts, Section 32 and 47 reports, psychologists interviewing you and your children, judges making orders, solicitors and barristers negotiating on the courthouse steps … all while you wait at number 78 or 79 on a list of perhaps 85 cases. There is no way an objective person would choose this option, but they would be someone who isn't entrenched in an acrimonious separation.

Plenty of parents separate without going through such battles. Somehow, they separate without any major tension and figure out shared parenting with ease. Well done to those people! The chances are, in such cases, there was no animosity and they were able to break up with limited conflict. The reasons are complex as to why some couples can do this. What unfolds after a breakup is influenced by the couple's personalities and their specific circumstances.

Conflict resolution wasn't part of the curriculum in school, nor was dealing with hurt and pain. We all feel differently for different reasons, and many people have experienced trauma prior to a breakup. Suffice to say, many people are already vulnerable when dealing with such matters through the courts. Parenting through a separation or divorce is complicated. Those who judge and cast aspersions should try to understand that these issues are difficult. In the real world, for people in Ireland today, parenting after divorce is far from simple.

Separation and divorce can put tremendous financial and emotional pressure on individuals. Even in cases where there is no financial pressure, there is often conflict, and this stress can be crippling. It is widely reported in the press and by government that the courts system is ineffective for families. This is commonly expressed by the people dealing with the courts system, who describe it as 'hell on earth', a sentiment I share wholeheartedly based on my experience. Going through a separation and divorce in the courts system was such an unpleasant experience that I can't possibly describe it. The worry, fear, and dread throughout this process can be mentally torturous. We cannot expect this not to have an adverse effect on our parenting. Being overwhelmed by stress doesn't mean we don't still love, adore, and want the best for our children – of course we do. However, when we are involved in a difficult court battle, we are regularly in fight-or-flight mode. Our automatic responses to conflict are not rational or considered. When we are stressed and under significant pressure, it is simply impossible to be the best parents we can be. Stress can make a person very ill, and putting stress on an ex-partner by being difficult will most definitely make parenting harder.

## Hurt People Hurt People

When a parent makes a degrading remark, demeans, or slags their child's other parent, they may as well have done this to the child. Reflect on this for a moment. On the whole, children feel themselves to be part of both their parents. From the time they were born, observations have been made about them having their mother's eyes and their father's nose. Our children grow up knowing they are part of us. They were created and moulded by us. If you wouldn't say something *about* your child, don't say it about their other parent in front of them. In doing so, you are taking a piece of that child and causing untold damage. We are kidding ourselves if we deny this. Explaining that you weren't aiming for the child is not good enough. If you don't want to hurt your children, put down your weapons.

Parents can try to distance a child from the battle they take on against their ex-spouse. However, the fact is that our children often feel what we feel. At the very least, they can sense what we are feeling. With the best will in the world, as much as we may believe that we are extremely disciplined and do not discuss the issues or make negative remarks in front of them, children often know instinctively when we are upset and dealing with difficult issues. It simply cannot be avoided that they are affected by this. Allowing solicitors to issue nasty letters to your ex-spouse and going for their blood in court impacts the whole household. Dragging your ex-spouse through the courts in a traumatic, expensive, litigious affair is, in my opinion, one of the worst things you could do for your child.

'But it's only my ex-spouse I have a problem with!' I hear you say. 'They are being unreasonable!'

If you really want to avoid hurting your children, reduce your own stress, and find a way forward in everyone's best interests, avoid the battle and look for an alternative resolution.

For a moment, let's focus on how to parent through the different stages of a breakup. Assume for a moment that we didn't need to hand over parenting decisions to the courts. Even if you have a case listed for court or have engaged solicitors, it is still possible to resolve conflict and create a parenting plan with the help of a neutral, experienced third party, who works with both parents in the best interests of the children.

## COMMUNICATION

Communication is one of the first things we learn when we come into the world, yet we struggle with it throughout our lives.

With any conflict comes difficulty surrounding communication. It goes with the territory. For any progress to be made, this needs to be addressed, preferably without blame and with a focus on the endgame.

Step one is accepting that communication with your ex-spouse is necessary to coparent effectively. If you and your ex-spouse communicate effectively and not through the children, that's great. If it's not broken, don't fix it.

Some parents have become used to not speaking to each other at all. They are in the habit of communicating through the children and, like any habit, this can be broken. Try to remember the greater good. Communicating with your ex-spouse is not a signal that their previous behaviour was acceptable or that you have forgiven them for the hurt. It is simply what is required. I understand that for some people, this seems pointless and difficult. Think of it like getting into the icy cold Irish Sea in December. Unless, of course, you're a sea swimmer, the thought of it is awful and, initially, it's painful … but once you're in, you can do it if you use the strokes you know. Yes, it's still cold – this doesn't go away. The Irish Sea will always be cold and you may never accept the behaviour of your ex-spouse as being anything other than cold (or worse), but you can still do this. The benefits of swimming in the cold sea are wonderful, as are the benefits of effective communication with your ex-spouse. Try to keep this in the forefront of your mind.

If communication has broken down completely, take the time to write a short email to your ex-spouse asking to resume communication around parenting. Be clear that it is only to address arrangements and/or the children's essential needs. Communication often breaks down when a party can no longer face a further battle. As part of the fight-or-flight response, this is a common and natural reaction to conflict, manifesting in many cases as no communication at all. Take that battle away, draw a line in the sand, and identify the exact issues on which you wish to communicate. Start small, identifying as few issues as possible. Select a form of communication with which both you and your ex-spouse are comfortable. If speaking results in a row, try texting or emailing. Treat this communication as you would in a professional context: be polite and deal in facts. Don't get personal or say anything you wouldn't to a colleague.

Construct your texts or emails in the same way each time, remembering to stick to the agreed upon items: times for drop-offs, items of clothing, or details of matches and activities. Always remain professional. Think of it like a baking recipe: baking calls for precise measurements, and leaving out or adding an ingredient risks ruining the outcome.

If you do communicate but find that it is tense and often ruptures into a row, give yourself a break from the stress. Put a plan in place. Suggest to your ex-partner that, to avoid ongoing stress, you stick to text or email for arrangements with a list of key topics. Ask for their suggestions to improve the situation. The likelihood is that you are both stressed due to the difficulties with communicating. It is very easy to get into arguments over text when trying to have our point heard and win an argument.

## A Communication Strategy

- Firstly, agree to draw a line in the sand.
- Admit that things haven't been effective and that you want them to improve.

- Suggest a communication plan and ask the other parent for their suggestions.
- Pick the essential topics on which you need to communicate. Keep the list short to begin with.
- Use email or text to communicate these topics.
- Always be polite.
- Make every effort to reply promptly.
- Stick to the agreed topics where at all possible.
- Keep it short and sweet. Be as clear as possible without being rude.
- Don't bring your emotions into things. This may take a concerted effort, but it will lead to better communication in the future. Treat it like you would a professional communication, in which you wouldn't consider detailing your emotions.
- Creating one space to communicate about your children can be very useful to begin with. Consider creating an email account specifically for discussing parenting arrangements.
- Be consistent. For coparenting to work, consistency is vital and is always in the best interests of the children.
- Be flexible too. As much as consistency is key, life calls for flexibility and it aways works both ways.

Remember that this is your most important job. A clear strategy and plan can only help to get it right.

Communication is only one part (albeit an essential part) of parenting. There are many more things to discuss. Again, we are all at different junctures on our journeys. Essentially, we all have some idea of what is best for our children and how we see their lives in the future. Some parents have a clear plan, others not so much. Some are just managing to get through the day and can't see any further ahead.

No matter where you are in your journey, my recommendation is to draw up a parenting plan with the help of an experienced family mediator. A professional family mediator will always work with couples in the best interests of their children, ensuring that the children's voices are heard throughout mediation and reflected in the parenting plan.

To create this plan, both parties should address what is really important to them and for the children. If you were to make a list, what would it look like? If both parties were to answer some questions on parenting, how far apart would your answers be?

The below list comprises parenting questions to be addressed before you draw up a plan. I recommend taking the time to think about your answers separately. Share and discuss your answers afterwards.

Many parents will be on the same page regarding parenting, which is great. Many others may have become entrenched in positions they believe to be in their children's best interests. In such cases, parents should seek help and consider the alternatives.

## PARENTING QUESTIONNAIRE

1.  How is parenting currently divided?
2.  How do you see the parenting structure going forward?
3.  Where do you wish for the children to be dropped off and collected when you are living separately?
4.  What communication is currently in place during the time you don't spend with your children?
5.  Is this communication working for you and the children? If not, how could it be improved?
6.  How important is the children's relationship with their grandparents on a scale of 1-10 (1 being extremely important, 10 being not at all important)?
7.  Do you favour a routine for the children?
    - Yes / No
8.  If so, what does that routine look like?
9.  Do you supervise the children's homework?
    - Yes / No
10. What is a suitable bedtime for the children?
    - Midweek _____ Weekends _____
11. How important is discipline in your children's lives? What does this look like to you?
12. In which extracurricular activities do the children partake? How important are these activities in your children's lives?

13. Do the children have extra or special needs that should be addressed? Please give details.
14. Have you any concerns about the other parent addressing these needs? If so, what are these concerns?
15. Which religious or other special occasions do you expect to celebrate in your child's life?
16. How do you see the sharing of special occasions going forward?
17. Do you have any concerns regarding the other parent taking the children on holidays, either within or outside of the country? If so, what are these concerns?
18. Have you discussed your separation with your children? Have you any thoughts on this?
19. Have you thought about introducing your children to a new partner? What are your concerns, if any, about this?
20. List any other concerns you may have around parenting going forward.

The way we parent is always evolving with our children's needs, growth, and development. It is important to be aware that plans pertaining to our children can and will change. As joint guardians, parents have joint responsibilities to their children and should be mindful of the rights afforded to them, as previously discussed. Putting our thoughts on paper or speaking to a professional are great places to start the process of creating a working parenting plan.

## CREATE A SUCCESSFUL PARENTING PLAN

- There is no better place to start than by identifying the issues on which both parents agree.
- Centre your plan around those agreed upon issues to begin with.
- Accept that the issues on which you currently disagree will need more work.
- Break up any difficult tasks into smaller pieces to make them more manageable.
- Make a list of the issues that need to be addressed and identify the positions of both parents on each matter.
- Look for alternative options. There is always an alternative.

- Reality test the different options.
- Bring the voice of the child into the room. However, I do not advise asking children to make difficult decisions. Take care not to put more on the children than is strictly necessary.

## TWO HOMES AFTER SEPARATION

Following parental separation, there is an adjustment period that can be a scary time for children. It is important to discuss this in mediation when making your parenting plan, as this a great place for parents to prepare themselves for the conversation with their children about their new living arrangements. If you have taken your child's voice and feelings into account when deciding on their new living arrangements, you will no doubt have already considered this important conversation. If you have not yet reached this stage, it is important for parents to be a united front when explaining the arrangements to children.

This may not be what children want to hear and it may take them by surprise. Some children may be too young to fully comprehend the situation. Whatever the case, children benefit when parents can agree upon a plan and present it to them. It may be helpful to involve children in the move, even if only in a small way. Perhaps they could help with the décor or planning the layout of a room. Let your children take part in the process in some small way.

Children should understand that where they spend most of their time is not based on who loves them the most. In an age-appropriate way, parents should explain that time with both parents is important and that the children are equally important to both parents. This is for the benefit of the children, not the parents. It is important to reassure children as clearly as possible about arrangements for school and afterschool activities. Explain in advance which nights they will spend with which parent and stick to this planned routine as much as possible.

## A WORK IN PROGRESS

Try to always focus on what is best for your children. It's all too easy for adults to get into a battle of wills, vying to achieve their own ideals. Separating parenting from other issues is not easy. Take any help you can get and remember that court battles should be the last resort.

'Children just want to be like everyone else.' These words were said to me by a very experienced child psychologist some years ago. They have always stuck with me, for it sounds so simple. If only we could just let our children feel 'like everyone else'. To me, that means children shouldn't feel the stress of their parents' separation. They shouldn't be afraid that a light will be shone on them at school, on the soccer pitch, or at their Communions or Confirmations. They shouldn't have to worry that anyone will view them differently. Parents inevitably impact whether this is possible for their children, and it is an important part of parenting to get right.

If mum and dad are okay, the children will be okay. This is easier said than done, but in instances where both parents have engaged in a process to create a plan and work together, they have started on the right path. If we as parents are already engaged in battle, it's a huge challenge to convince our children that we are okay. Consider the following practical tips to help yourself through this difficult time.

## Practical Tips

Look after yourself: put your own seatbelt on first. You are of no use to anyone if you're not well.

Acknowledge that your mental health is under stress when dealing with your separation or divorce, and plan accordingly.

Your first step may be preparing yourself to deal with the problems between you and your ex-partner. This preparation might be as simple as reminding yourself not to react.

Reduce your stress. It is unrealistic to expect to be able to deal with ongoing stress without it having an impact on you.

Take time out to clear your head, even if it is only a thirty-minute walk before collecting the children.

When faced with conflict, don't respond immediately; count down from ten before reacting.

When parenting, it's important to remember that it isn't about us; it's about our children. Key to this is remembering that our children are part of both parents. Children have fundamental rights: to be loved and to be free from the stress of their parents' divorce. When we are tempted to dig our heels in, we need to consider how our children are feeling. How might this worry be experienced by a ten-year-old child, for instance? Put yourself in your child's shoes. Who wants their child to feel heartbreak or pain, to feel like they aren't enough for their parents, or to think their parents won't put them first? Heartbreak is just as painful for children as it is for adults. Don't do it to them. You may recognise that you're struggling and that your children are overhearing inappropriate comments. In this case, perhaps you could try these tips.

## PARENTING TIPS

- Never use your children as messengers.
- As a rule, don't vent in front of your children.
- Don't jump to conclusions when children come home with stories after their time with the other parent. Children dealing with conflict quickly learn how to elicit reactions and attention. Take some time to process what you have heard and don't react too hastily.
- Don't push buttons. We all know how to do this to our ex-spouses. Making a conscious decision not to do so benefits the children.
- Don't be afraid to ask for help.
- Give yourself some time out from parenting alone, even if it's only a short break.
- Let the little things go.

## THE IMPOSSIBLE PARENT

Some people believe they can be a parent without doing any actual parenting. While they may be a parent in the biological or legal sense, you and your children may have been repeatedly let down by such a person. In your heart and soul, you know you're not putting any obstacles in the way. You have made excuses for their absence in the hope that things will improve. There seems to be no reason for the no-shows. Time and time again, your child is left disappointed.

This situation happens all over the world and it's hard for the children involved. Unfortunately, the courts cannot force a parent to see their child and neither can you. This is an awful situation for any parent to navigate. However, be mindful that you are in control of your own actions. We cannot change the behaviour of the parent who won't take responsibility, who instead leaves it on your shoulders. This is extremely hard to accept. For anyone who has not experienced this situation, it is impossible to understand the hurt we feel for our hurting children. The natural reaction is, of course, to lash out, get cross, and vent, and no one would blame you.

At this time, it is necessary to show strength, rise above the situation, and focus your energy on yourself and your children. Try to keep your focus and not get caught up in anger. Wherever you can, accept help from those around you. Shelter your children from the absence of their missing parent for as long as possible. When it is for the greater good, it is okay to tell white lies to smaller children. Though no one might thank you now, they will in time, and in the meantime it's okay to say to yourself: 'Well done, you.' When the time is right and your child is a young adult, you can make the decision to have an honest conversation with them. Remember: it's not their fault and neither is it yours.

Remember why you had children in the first place and keep in mind your dreams and aspirations for them. As parents, we are making memories for our children's futures. Let's focus on as many good ones as we can. Parents are only human and we all make mistakes. If you haven't had a good day, that's okay. Chalk it down to experience and try again tomorrow.

# 8

## SELF-CARE

Taking care of ourselves has never been so prominently discussed on our TVs, in magazines, or on our social media feeds. We have all we need to know about the latest health and wellness trends at our fingertips. One thing that won't be in your social media feed, however, is how stressful the journey of a separation or divorce really is. It's certainly not a widely recognised grief. It is rare for a divorce not to be an extremely traumatic event in a person's life, yet there is no time off work in recognition of this. There is no doctor with a magic pill that can take away the hurt and pain that comes with a marriage breakdown.

In Ireland, there is a huge need to talk about marriage breakdown, to recognise how it affects us, and to discuss how it should be dealt with. It is the one thing for which we won't receive community support. A sense of shame still very much exists around marriage breakdown.

Months and sometimes years of planning go into our weddings in Ireland. Weddings are a big business here: the most popular hotels have long waiting lists and it is no mean feat to book a makeup artist for the big day. Suited and booted grooms and their blushing brides invite their nearest and dearest to celebrate their love. We save, borrow, and spend fortunes to have the nicest flowers, the prettiest dresses, and the best champagne, wine, and food we can offer. We spend sleepless nights on our speeches to express our love and devotion in front of our special guests. So much time goes into selecting the perfect song to reflect just how much we love each other.

Is it any wonder that, after a marriage breakdown, we feel broken ourselves? The feelings of despair and loss can be overwhelming. We worry about our children and have mixed feelings about what is best for them. We feel guilty for not giving them the family life that we had envisioned. This can be extremely difficult for people to come to terms with.

The journey to reaching the endpoint of a relationship looks different for everyone. For many people, marriage has been long and difficult, and the end was long overdue. For others, the end came on foot of a betrayal. For some people, it came as a shock, as they didn't see it coming. I have spoken to people who are hurt and betrayed, people who wish with all their heart that things were different. I have seen people who don't want to think about things at all. They just want to get on with things quickly so as not to feel. I have seen people self-destruct and self-sabotage. Finding a way to process everything we are dealing with in a divorce is different for everyone. There is no map, no exact guide. It is important to take the time to allow yourself to heal.

## MY JOURNEY

On my journey, navigating and processing the pain came in the form of regular long walks in the forest, a twelve-kilometre loop near where I lived. I took myself, my head full of hurt, and my shattered heart there a few times a week. I had no real intentions at the time, but I knew I had to move my body. I would drop the girls to creche and school before getting myself to the forest, so that I could keep it together enough to make lunches, sign homework journals, and hug and kiss my children. I did what I had to do. But my two feet were heavy, my Asics runners like bricks on my feet. Driving into the school carpark, smiling at the other parents, and getting away as quickly as possible was my morning routine.

In the forest, tears poured down my face and no one noticed. It was a painful and personal journey. I grew up without a set plan for my life: I didn't map out my marriage or having my children. But I had done those things and I loved them so much. They were my life and I had given everything to them. I gave even more because I carried so much guilt surrounding my first broken marriage. I couldn't have tried harder to make a happy home, build a business, make memories, and give my children the very best. I cooked, I cleaned, I made money, and had done my best to look well. I took care of myself, going to the gym after I had my babies and making sure I wasn't fat. I had gone as far as thinking that I looked okay. I had tried to listen to my partner and understand how he felt. I tried to figure out why he wasn't happy and how to be a good wife. I wanted desperately for my children not to have a broken home.

My inner self had always struggled with believing that I was good enough. That was part of me – I carried it for years. Now, the devastation of having failed was so hard. It was killing me that my marriage was over. My feelings of failure were palpable, as was the idea that I was failing my children. I was traumatised, that much I recognised. As I walked, I cried. When I finished, I tried to leave behind the sadness and the inner voice that berated me for what I could and should have done differently. One foot in front of the other, I kept going. There was never a plan. It helped to feel sad and sorry for myself for a while as I walked through the woods, thinking about all that was gone. Deciding to leave it all there helped me to function for the rest of the day.

At some point, I recognised that I wasn't to blame. My time away from that voice (and the person who made me feel so bad about my very presence) was helping me to heal. It took a long time for me to realise that I was going to be okay. It wasn't done and dusted. It's a long pathway from wanting to lie down and die, wishing you could just disappear, to recognising that you can go forward and begin to feel better. There were many peaks and troughs. Clearing a space allows you to reconnect with yourself and with your instinct – that guide that worked intuitively before. When you are very quiet, you can hear it: your inner voice, your instinct, your gut. We all have it. But we sometimes can't – or don't – listen. In my case, I didn't listen, for I was dealing with shame and wanted to repair something quickly. I was in a painful place and with the wrong person. I had put my energy into something that didn't match it. Working on listening to our inner voice – that instinct we all have – is an important part of rediscovering ourselves. To be in a position where we can listen to that inner voice, we must deal with and process our trauma and hurt.

For a moment, think of a time when you were led by your instinct, when you listened to it and followed it. Not when you followed your ego, were led by guilt, or were bullied into a decision. A time when your instinct told you to buy that house, to take that job, to say yes to an invitation, or to follow a particular direction in life. It worked out well because you listened to what was right for you. Instinctively, it was right. What were the circumstances of those choices? Who was around you? What were you doing in your life at the time? Recognise these things and you will be where you are supposed to be. Learning to listen can come and go, and we can easily get distracted.

It is a cathartic feeling when you learn to be okay with having been hurt, and when you can appreciate the lessons learnt and be thankful. I know, I know; it entirely depends at what point you ask yourself to be accepting and grateful. At some stages, it seems inconceivable to be grateful for the hurt.

'Who the hell would want that – are you completely mad?' I hear you say. But if you allow yourself to feel the hurt and if you can put it down, the anger will subside and your tears will dry. You know you'll be okay. You will live another day.

You now have a choice to make. You know you don't have to make the same mistake again. You can recognise it and let go. It's a choice. If you have done the work, acknowledged the hurt, and let it out, you can be grateful for the lessons learnt. Find your peace; it does exist. It exists in our children, the greatest loves of our lives, the parts of us that are walking, living, breathing miracles. From these lessons, we know more about ourselves. We have learned what wasn't meant for us. We can decide to breathe on our own and move on. Bitterness is only bitter for us. It is the taste in our mouths should we choose to remain in the moment.

## A GOOD PLACE TO START

The first step is accepting that divorce and separation are traumatic, life-changing events, though they are of course experienced differently for different people, whose relationships and personalities differ.

The word 'separate' means to disconnect. Disconnecting can feel very isolating, and isolation can have a very negative impact on a person, especially when combined with grief. Very often in breakups, one person becomes more isolated than the other, as many people take sides. Depression may set in due to the sadness and pain. People may choose to self-isolate to avoid dealing with their grief in the outside world. This is all too common and can lead to addiction, self-sabotage, rage, chronic fatigue, and further depression.

Following a breakup, we go through several stages. It is crucial that we understand what we are dealing with so we know how to help ourselves. To help us get to the other side, we need the right tools to deal with the anger and hurt, as well as compassion throughout this difficult time.

## RECOGNISING GRIEF

Real grief follows the breakdown of a marriage. Grief is the emotional reaction to loss and the acute pain that accompanies it, whether that is the loss of a loved one or a thing that was loved deeply. There is no place to go to mourn the death of a marriage, which is so much more than no longer being with your spouse. Gone are all your dreams and plans for your future together; they have come to an end. Losing the life you had with that person causes intense pain.

If you willingly made the choice to end your marriage, your journey is different. People who mourned the death of their relationship whilst still married will be at a different stage by the time they separate from their spouse. Most of us will go through various stages, whether or not we choose to recognise them.

Many people dealing with divorce are going through what is known as 'disenfranchised grief'. This is when grief is kept hidden and not dealt with, which can be very difficult for people struggling to come to terms with the loss of their marriage. We in Ireland still live in a predominately Catholic country, where many people undoubtedly carry guilt and shame. Having been taught to get on with life when it's difficult, they don't deal with trauma or grief, only to bottle up these feelings for later.

## The Five Stages of Divorce Grief

It is hugely important for our mental health to recognise grief for what it is. If we can do so, this awareness enables us to deal with our grief and learn to accept it.

1. **Denial**
   Divorce can be chaotic. Oftentimes, one or both parties hold onto hope that the breakup isn't real. As it can be extremely hard to contemplate the turmoil ahead, people may hold onto the belief that they can fix things, trying to convince themselves that the situation is not real.
2. **Anger**
   We need anger: it is an important, natural feeling that stops us from falling apart. Though we mustn't use it in a negative way by taking things out on others, we should recognise that it's okay to feel angry.
3. **Bargaining**
   This is the stage at which one goes back to see what can be done, to try again before the inevitable happens. This is often met with rejection, which can lead to overwhelming feelings of loneliness.
4. **Depression**
   At this stage, people often feel overwhelmingly sad and hopeless.
5. **Acceptance**
   This is when we fully understand that there is no going back.

Though people may want to know how long each stage will last, there is no specific timeframe, as it is different for everyone. However, the longer the relationship, the longer the grieving period will likely last.

## LONELINESS

As discussed, the journey through divorce and its aftermath is different for everyone. Those who were in difficult relationships may have become isolated even before the breakup. They may have become distanced from their families or found it impossible to maintain friendships due to a controlling or abusive partner. Although some people find it comforting to spend time alone, others find loneliness deeply painful. Changing this situation requires a push. It's tough but it can only come from you. To begin this change, decide to do one small thing outside of your comfort zone.

For people who are isolated in small towns and villages throughout the country, it can take planning not to be alone, which isn't easy. Putting yourself out there can be uncomfortable but it is worthwhile. Start by making a plan: write down some of the things you want to do and follow up by finding out what's available in your area.

Try reaching out to an old friend with whom you've lost touch. Arrange to meet up with someone who makes you laugh. Join a group - there are running, walking, and book clubs out there, among others. If these aren't available in your area, ask a few neighbours if they would like to start one with you. Pick a funny book that everyone will enjoy. You may be surprised to realise you're not the only one who could benefit from some company. Socialising will distract you from your thoughts and help you on your journey.

## BE COMPASSIONATE

There is no magic pill for dealing with emotional pain. While some of us hope it will just go away, others choose to share. One thing is for sure: we should treat ourselves with compassion. If the person dealing with this grief was your brother, sister, or best friend, what would you offer them? Buckets of compassion and as much support as you could muster! Do the same for yourself. Be kind and say only kind things, the same as you would to anyone else who was hurting. Forbid negative self-talk, do nice things for yourself, and spoil yourself when you can. Tread softly; this is a tricky journey.

## Do Talk

Letting your feelings out is important; venting is healthy. Finding the right person to talk to is also important. In the initial stages of a breakup, we often share our feelings with our close loved ones, but we quickly realise that they too become emotional and upset. We don't wish to cause more upset so we shut down. The emotional turmoil of a marriage breakdown can spread stress throughout the wider family unit.

Venting to a pragmatic friend, who will just listen to us without trying to fix things, may be just what is needed. Many people attend counselling for support during their difficult divorce journeys. Counselling can equip us with techniques to better manage negative feelings, while also helping to address unresolved issues in a safe and caring environment.

## Meditation

Your mind, body, soul, and spirit are all interconnected. Whether you believe this or not, I know it for sure; it's just how we are made.

I think that, for many of us, spirituality always meant having a crystal ball and believing in ghosts. I have always questioned what life is all about; as a child, I never stopped asking questions. It's no wonder I was told that children should be seen and not heard – it was the only way Dad could get me to stop talking! I wanted to know what more there was to life and where we came from. To some degree, I still do.

It wasn't until I visited a craniosacral therapist (due to suffering with Bell's palsy) that I realised the full power of the mind-body-soul-spirit connection. When we are out of sorts from dealing with difficulties in our lives, the connection between these elements is perhaps not looked after and therefore not working well. To help our minds, bodies, souls, and spirits, there are things we can do to balance ourselves. In times of stress, we need to do this more than ever.

Dr Russell Jaffe, an expert in this field, explains the connection as follows:

'There is a gut nervous system and a central nervous system, and they are always in communication in a very intimate communion. His Holiness the Dali Lama has gotten together a group of scientists and advanced meditating monks, and at the first meeting some thirty years ago, he said the monks were going to learn science and the scientists were going to learn to meditate. So it's not an academic exercise when we talk about staying with your breath as a refuge. Learn how to breathe, and when you're under stress, keep breathing. It's more complicated than that, but if you want to lower your stress cortisol and raise your healthy DHEA (a biomarker of stress), if you want to lower your stress adrenal and raise your serotonin, if you want to have a healthy neurochemistry in your brain, in your gut, and in your body, keep breathing. It's a very important component of the human stress response. When we know how to keep breathing under stress, we can release moment my moment, breath by breath, what would already accumulate within us as a stressfully neurohormonal response.'

Practising mindfulness and greater awareness can help. We can choose to keep breathing. We can meditate and help ourselves to breathe. We can centre and focus ourselves.

## EXPRESS GRATITUDE

I know, don't shoot me: this is about getting through your divorce – and no, I'm not watching too much Oprah (and yes, I wanted to shoot my ex-husband too – I jest!). Humour me for just a moment. What harm can it do to try? Every successful coach from Tony Robbins to Brene Browne to Echart Tolle can't say enough about practising gratitude. Give it a try; start yourself on a journey. Spend ten minutes before bed thinking about five things for which you are grateful. Involve your children by giving them a little notepad so you can do it as a family. If you commit to those ten minutes, soon you'll be thinking about which five things you can write down. If you start to voice your gratitude, before you know it, you will subconsciously be feeling grateful for all that you have. Try to really feel it. Remember that it's impossible to feel sad when you're feeling grateful. It's too easy to list our woes and feel sorry for ourselves, whereas practising gratitude teaches us to count our blessings. The more blessings you count, the better. While this won't make your problems go away, focusing on the positive can help us through the difficult times.

## EXERCISE

Exercise is important, yet it can be the hardest thing to do when you are suffering mentally and emotionally. However, it is during these times that you need it more than ever.

Ten benefits of exercise on mental health:

- Sharper memory and thinking
- Higher self-esteem
- Better sleep
- More energy
- Greater resilience
- Helps fight depression
- Increased happiness
- Increased productivity
- Helps maintain a healthy weight

Without taking on too much, do some exercise. This doesn't have to mean rearranging your life. Don't let yourself opt out. Even if it's only twenty minutes, put the runners in the car or go for a walk. You won't regret prioritising daily exercise. If you do miss a few days, that's okay - get back out there! If you decide to fit your exercise into your morning routine, get yourself organised. If you leave it to the last minute, you may not do it.

## A HEALTHY DIET

Without wishing to state the obvious, when we're under stress, it's all too easy to avoid looking after ourselves. If we eat rubbish, we feel rubbish. (Where have we heard that before?) In all the chaos of a divorce, we often put our needs aside, but now more than ever, you need to avoid adding to your stress. Looking after your diet is so important: a healthy diet is good not only for your physical health, but for your mental health too. Processed foods are linked to depression, as is alcohol.

## NURTURING RELATIONSHIPS

Fostering friendships during this time is so important. Though you need support, people aren't mind-readers or therapists, so reach out to friends and family. We are social creatures for whom social interaction is extremely important. Friendships hugely benefit our mental health and wellbeing.

Friends of both halves of a separating couple may feel torn and have divided loyalties. Some may have sided with your partner. This is to be expected; it is not unusual. While it may be difficult, it is not worth adding this to your stress. Rise above the desire to engage in tit-for-tat and don't badmouth your ex. Ultimately, treat others how you would like to be treated. If others choose to judge based on half a story, let them.

# 9

## LIFE AFTER DIVORCE

### AN INTRODUCTION

You have been traumatised. Whichever form of hellish torture you have endured will depend on the route you took to divorce. You've been through the mindboggling nightmare of the Irish family court system and now you're an expert on coparenting with nothing to show for it but guilt and stress. You've suffered judgement from people who know nothing about your divorce or your life with your ex-partner. Your dreams and plans for the future have been eviscerated. But you're still standing.

### GETTING YOUR MOJO BACK

Isn't it about time you got your mojo back? This is what I called the 'get out of jail' feeling. That may be slightly dramatic but my experience was truly a slow form of torture. The letters, the waiting, the solicitors who refused to return a phone call, the lies, more lies, the reports, being told that my ex-husband and his girlfriend would make decisions ... okay, enough. I'm not living there anymore. I'm done with living there! It's time to shift your mindset and enjoy the next chapter in your life.

There has to be a moment where you say, 'Enough! I've cried a river or two and I'm done. There is a whole world out there just waiting for me!' Perhaps you have the restrictions of real life and the whole world might wait a while, but let's start with one night every other week or maybe the odd weekend. Maybe you don't have those kinds of restrictions and you can do the whole *Eat, Pray, Love* experience. (I highly recommend the book and the film if you haven't read or seen them.) It's time to find your mojo – do you remember a time when you had yours? Do you remember having a spring in your step before the weight of the world fell on you? Think back to the time before you became someone you didn't recognise, when you had and did things that you enjoyed. What made you laugh and light up? What did you enjoy? Getting this back may take some motivation but you can do it! Get the haircut, put on the lippie, buy the new runners, do some exercise, play your music, climb the mountain! Maybe buy a bike or go sea swimming. Grab the girls and guys and go out. It may require more planning now – so be it! The old haunts may have changed and you might need to find an age-appropriate venue, but just get out! Invite people over – when did you last entertain? Who doesn't enjoy entertaining? Dress the house and yourself and have a laugh. If you're reading this, you're not dead, and if you're not dead, go out there and find that mojo – it's just for you!

## LEARN TO LOVE YOURSELF

I understand this one isn't so easy, but you can and should learn to love yourself. It's imperative. This task really depends on the level of rubbish (I don't want to curse!) you've put up with for the past few years. Regardless of whether you want to lay eyes on another partner for the rest of your life, learning to love yourself is important for your wellbeing. You are the person you will spend all your time with, so if you want good company, learn to love yourself as a first step. I'm not talking about arrogance or being full of yourself, but the need to create self-esteem and confidence and leave the negative self-talk in the past.

Remember:

1. Stop all criticism of yourself and others. Begin now. Once you decide to do this, stick to it. You wouldn't be mean to your child or a loved one, so don't do it to yourself.
2. Start talking positively to yourself. It might sound strange but it's a commitment to your success and wellbeing.
3. Practise telling yourself in the mirror every day that you love yourself. Don't take this one too seriously. When I think about it, I always think of my granddad talking to himself in the mirror, combing his few strands of hair and fixing his fedora whilst telling himself he was a 'handsome brute'. I think he may have done it to amuse us, but really it was a practice of self-love that we should all emulate!

## JOURNALING

When you were younger, you may have kept a diary to keep track of all your thoughts (or to confess who you didn't like or what trouble you were in). It felt good to get your thoughts down on paper and it was considered healthy.

Keeping a journal as an adult can have many benefits. Simply writing down your thoughts can help with planning and creating order when times are changing. On your new journey, it can help you get to know yourself more, to know your thoughts, fears, and feelings. It keeps your brain in shape and helps with processing overwhelming emotions. It can help to manage anxiety, reduce stress, and cope with depression. Journaling helps to control your symptoms and improve your mood by enabling you to prioritise problems, fears, and concerns. Tracking day-to-day symptoms helps with recognising triggers so you can find ways to better control them.

## PARENTING AFTER DIVORCE

With a parenting plan already in place, you're doing your best to work with it. This might be a greater challenge than you realised, and it is different for everyone. Oftentimes, the 'firsts' are the hardest: the first weekend your child is away from you, the first time they lose a tooth and you weren't there, or the first holiday they spend without you. Make a plan for yourself for the nights your child isn't going to be with you. You don't have to paint the town red – just make sure you stay occupied. Dwelling on things and allowing yourself to feel sad won't do you any good. Fill this time with something positive that you can't do when the children are around. Accept that this is time for the other parent to spend with the children. It's not time that you can manage. There should be a specified time in your parenting agreement for you to check in with the children; stick to this. You will already have agreed that, should any serious issue arise, such as a medical issue, both parents are each other's first port of call. Let go of what the children might be doing or eating. Now that parenting is being shared, you are not the one doing the parenting when the children aren't with you.

It can be difficult for everyone involved when children are introduced to a parent's new partner. Let's be clear: what you or your former partner do in your own time and who you choose to date is your own business. For many separated people, the idea of an ex-spouse moving on can't come quickly enough. However, our children being introduced to the new person in our ex's life is something to be treated with respect and consideration. Doing so in a mindful manner will have rewards for all going forward.

## Things to Consider

Assess whether your new relationship is advanced enough for your partner to meet your children.

Now more than ever, stability in your child's life is important, as they have already been through a big change.

Be sure to let the children and the other parent know in advance that you will be introducing a new partner. Let them know what is going on.

Make the introduction incrementally, a little at a time.

Ultimately, think about how you would like to be told about someone new in your children's lives and have the same consideration for your ex-spouse.

## A STATE OF MIND

Your state of mind refers to your mood or mental state. There is a great variety of mental states, including perception, thought, belief, desire, intention, perception, outlook, and attitude. All of these are related to our state of mind.

Although our state of mind is affected by circumstances outside of our control, it is key to realise that we can make positive changes to our state of mind. We have the ability to create our own happiness and positive feelings, which can help us to feel the way we want to feel and to get to where we want to be in life.

## BRAIN POWER

Understanding the impact of positive thinking, positive affirmations, and 'mind over matter' can be lifechanging, enabling us to change our state of mind and therefore our lives. This understanding is available to all of us.

Don't get me wrong: when you're in the midst of a legal battle with your ex-spouse and there are solicitors' fees to be paid, children to be collected, and then something else goes wrong, you can feel sick with stress. Physically unable to reply with coherent thoughts, the state you are in is referred to as 'fight-or-flight'. In this state, our responses are incoherent. Neuroscientists can explain this in a very complicated way, involving discussions of physiology, intention, elevated emotions, and magnetic fields.

Here's my take on what's really important for the next chapter in your life: firstly, you must believe that you can change your thoughts from sadness to happiness, from shame to pride, from regret to hope, from resentful to content, and from being afraid to refusing to live in fear.

Think of it as a recipe for a cake that you love. Let's say a Victoria sponge made with the best quality butter, eggs, sugar, and flour, filled with homemade raspberry jam and fresh cream, dusted with icing sugar on top. Imagine that the sponge is baked to perfection: light and fluffy. Do as the recipe states in terms of the ingredients, the method, and the cooking time, and it will turn out well for you to enjoy. As with many recipes, you may have to try it numerous times before you get it right, but that's fine – so be it. Some of us might think we can't bake but we can all follow a recipe; it may just take a few more times until you get the right result. Use the recipe as many times as you need. As time passes, you may start to remember it by heart, eventually making it without even thinking about the list of ingredients, the method, or how to put it all together. Perhaps you forget about it from time to time, forgetting how nice it was, but you can take out the recipe book whenever you need it.

We know we're not really baking a cake here. The cake is a metaphor for the reward that follows taking the right steps to achieve our desired state of mind; the pleasant state of mind, the one that's not full of hate, fear, or resentment. Who wants to feel like that? Life shouldn't be this hard, and it doesn't have to be, so let's figure this out.

Neuroscience now tells us that we have three brains, or perhaps three parts to our brain, controlling different matters and functions. These three elements of the brain can take us from thinking to doing to being.

The first brain is the neocortex, which is the walnut-shaped structure that sits on the outside. This is the decision-making part of the brain. The limbic brain is about the size of a lemon and controls emotion and motivation, while the reptilian brain controls instincts and urges.

The neocortex is the seat of your conscious awareness, which refers to information you are taking in at the present moment. This part of the brain loves to gather information and, as it learns, it forges new connections within the brain, building information. The function of this brain is to learn and store, and in doing so, it enables us to remember. Our brain works hard to store information on a daily basis. When this information hits our five senses, the second part of the brain reacts. This isn't a thinking part of the brain, but the chemical brain.

Memories are experiences that we can remember: your first kiss or an outing for a fabulous meal, the taste of which you can still recall (along with the bill). These are all memories. If that bill was a surprise in that fancy, overpriced restaurant, you perked up and paid attention, which is why you can remember it in such detail. That event is called a memory.

Stress is when your body is knocked out of balance. When you see a lion, your primitive nervous system becomes engaged. It doesn't have to be a lion: it could be the thought of a memory stored in the neocortex, as stress can be brought on by thoughts alone. When such a memory enters your unconscious mind, the body does not know the difference between actual danger and the thought of danger. As far as your body is concerned, you are in danger, so the limbic brain reacts, beginning to make neuropeptides and signalling to the hormonal centres. This causes you to get a rush of energy to prepare you for an event, whether this is real or imagined. When this happens, you are altered in some way, as you enter the fight-or-flight state. Your pupils become dilated, you get a rush of blood, and your heart rate changes, as your body prepares for battle as you decide to stay and fight or to run.

Metacognition is how we can modify our reactions. At this stage, it is important to realise that our reactions can be stopped by the way we think. We first need to observe how the brain has responded based on the information it has built up. We can decide on the reaction we want to exhibit and keep these thoughts going to the brain. These are the pieces of knowledge we need to give to the brain to enable us to change our mind. You can begin to create coherence, which are new thoughts. If you persist with new thoughts and ideas, they are going to stick; they actually stick scientifically to your brain. Your effort is needed to stop, observe, recognise, and concentrate on your new thoughts, which we must keep generating and pushing so that, eventually, the old thoughts disappear. This is the science of changing your mind.

Next, your behaviour needs to match your intentions. For your actions to equal your thoughts, the mind and body must work together. The moment that happens, you feel content. Knowledge is for the mind and experience is for the body. Therefore, you emotionally teach your body with the information that the mind understands intellectually. You change your own makeup, your own fabric, when teaching your body to chemically understand what the mind intellectually knows. You need to do it over and over again, so many times you no longer have to think about it. You neurochemically condition the body, as well as the conscious mind, to memorise the feeling of being content. When this happens, the mind and body are working together, causing the cerebellum (the third brain) to be activated. The seat of the subconscious brain, this is the part associated with habit – things you don't have to think about but know how to do (though you don't necessarily know how you know!). It's automatic. Repetition can change the subconscious mind, meaning this third part of the brain kicks in because you've pushed hard. Becoming good at something usually takes a lot of effort, but once you master this repetition and successfully change your habits, you can alter the person you are.

All of this starts with us. It is possible for us to understand the above scientific explanation, along with how our own lives are influenced by our experiences. We are not in this state of mind all the time and we are all at different levels, depending on our experiences.

The important part is to understand what is going on within our bodies and brains, and why this causes us to react in the way we do to different situations. If we can reduce our stress and understand our brains a bit better, we know we can make positive changes.

## MY TAKE ON ATTRACTION

On the subject of the brain, I truly believe we can learn a lot from the law of attraction if we understand that we can control what we bring into our lives. You attract energies and people with whom you are in harmony. What does this mean in practice? The thoughts that you control give you the energy that you feel. What you attract depends on that energy. If you change your vibration and your energy, you can change your life.

When you feel negative and are in bad form, you will only attract negative energies – so become positive! Of course, it is not that easy, which takes us back to the subject of gratitude. Remember that it's impossible to feel pain when you're practising gratitude. All of this stems back to the power of the brain to change our subconscious. Now you must learn to use it to attract the things you want into your life.

If you change your subconscious brain, you can change how you behave and what you feel. You are in charge of your thoughts. When you wake up, you can decide to tell yourself that you're going to have a great day. In this way, our thoughts determine how the day will be. You can therefore think yourself out of a bad day; this is where 'fake it till you make it' comes into play. Get your brain into gear and tell yourself you're going to have a great day. Start there and soon you'll realise it works. Negative things pass and you will keep going. You will wake up and go again.

There are so many opportunities in your new life after divorce. Your choices will dictate how you feel and what you experience going forward. You are the only one who can decide whether to move on or stay stuck. Your power is in learning that you are the driving force in getting the things you want in life.

My favourite concepts regarding the law of attraction:

- You are a magnet: like attracts like.
- The negative will draw the negative, while the positive will draw the positive.
- If you are nice to people, nice people will be drawn to you.
- If you can see it in your mind, you can hold it in your hand.
- Visualise what you want; perhaps write it down in a notebook.
- Gratitude is powerful.
- Laughter attracts joy and releases negativity.
- Joy and depression cannot reside in the same place.
- You have not because you ask not.
- Write down the vision and make it plain.

## DATING AFTER DIVORCE

Do you remember Cilla Black's dating show, *Blind Date*? The host's matchmaking skills, the idea of the love match, willing the right person to be picked ... oh, I loved it! Nowadays, it's *Love Island*: young, attractive models with fit and fabulous bodies create unrealistic expectations of love for the viewers tuning in to see the latest match.

My first dating story after divorce was a light relief. Nothing was planned, it was just a good old-fashioned eyes-met-across-the-bar event. The few drinks on board provided the initial flow that the conversation needed and, without any expectations, dating commenced. Looking back, by this point, I was over the car-crash trauma of my marriage breakdown and had settled into a life of raising my girls. My mojo was returning. I was content and in a happy place with myself.

My new relationship was so much fun and we truly had a connection like nothing I'd experienced before. I hadn't thought much about whether I'd meet someone and fall in love again, or if I'd have another man on bended knee. But I did; it happened again. He proposed and I accepted. I had another sparkly ring on my finger, another wedding to plan, and another man wanting another baby. Stop – no way! Yes, I know: what the heck?! My double-barrel names were already stretched to capacity. My notions to myself were that all my second names were very aristocratic, but at this point I was pushing it. No, there was no chance. Zero. There wasn't a hope of me giving birth again; not on your nellie! (And not just because I couldn't have a child with *another* surname.) Not a chance, not for all the diamonds in Ireland. However, even without a son and an heir, it was a love story that would give Romeo and Juliet a run for their money. Mind you, someone ended up dead in that romantic tale and no one died in mine (which could have been by sheer luck). Maybe we were more like Bonnie and Clyde or *Lady and the Tramp* – yes, that's the one!

Dating and falling in love is different in each decade of life. When you've been through more rubbish than the local landfill, something in you switches and you know you don't have to take the crap anymore. As much as I'd love to spill the tea, that's a tale for another day. What I will say is that, when dating at – let's call it – a different stage in life, you have less tolerance for bullshit. That's the end of that story for now.

By this stage of my life, I have learned a lot about myself. I have learned a lot about dating, and I have learned I have a weakness for a man on bended knee. I know I see the best in people and I'm slow to test realities.

Dating is as much about your feelings for yourself as your feelings for the other person. The moral of the story is to be happy with yourself and the rest will follow. For the purposes of covering all bases, the following is some information on the wonderful world of modern dating.

## A Look at Dating Options

I know that for many newly single divorcées, the thought of dating again can make them cringe, but let's investigate how we go about dating now. There are so many dating apps available at our fingertips, from Tinder, which is free to join, to the costly Luxy dating app, styled as an elite dating site for millionaires. This one charges hundreds of euros just to sign up! There are also in-person dating agencies that charge an eyewatering €1,000 for a few vetted dates.

Unsurprisingly, Tinder is one of the most popular dating apps in the world. Even Brad Pitt mentioned Tinder in his acceptance speech at the Screen Actors Guild Awards, joking that he would 'add his award to his Tinder profile'.

The website 'Dating Zest' has some interesting stats on Tinder. Reportedly, the app has over 75 million users (wow!), of which 78 per cent are men, 22 per cent are women, and 30 per cent are married people. Registered on the app every day are more than 1.6 billion left and right swipes, as well as over 30 million matches, with overall matches totalling more than 60 billion. Tinder made $1.2 billion in 2020 from its paid subscribers, who number over 6 million. Though it is the most popular dating app in the USA, Tinder is also available in over 190 countries and in 30 languages. Interestingly, 'Dating Zest' advises that users tend to get the most matches on Monday evenings from 6 p.m. to 9 p.m. Quite shockingly, users spend on average 90 minutes per day swiping on Tinder. This dating app is predominantly used by a younger age bracket, with over 83 per cent of its users aged 16-34 and only 1 per cent of its users being over 55.

From these figures, we see that Tinder is clearly a roaring financial success with a total direct revenue of $1.79 billion, as reported in 2022. Another hugely successful enterprise is McDonalds, whose 2022 turnover was reportedly over $23.18 billion. However, we all know deep down that McDonalds isn't good for us, that there is far healthier, unprocessed food available. Documentaries have shown the poor health outcomes of eating from this mega successful franchise, yet we still eat it, promise never to go back, and still do. Similarly, Netflix's documentary *The Tinder Swindler* revealed the con of all cons stemming from the famous swiping app. Of course, no one believes it can happen to them. The point is: just because something is hugely financially successful doesn't mean it's good for us.

What with Tinder and *Love Island*, a lot has changed in the dating world and there appear to be many downsides associated with our modern lives. For instance, we can now throw away a relationship because the next one is available with the download of an app. On our screens, we see retouched pictures taken for social media, which fuel our desire for the unachievable. It can't be good for our relationships to see people with perfect bodies and perfect lives online. As with so many things in life, we change and so will the way we date. Hopefully, we will learn that all that glitters is not gold; the grass is not always greener. Moving on to the next relationship is not always what we anticipated. Of course, it's our choice to make. Breaking up is hard – it is seldom anything else. However, life doesn't have to be hard and dating again can be a lot of fun.

## EVERYTHING IS GOING TO BE OKAY

It's a lovely feeling – a content, happy, relaxed feeling – when you know you're going to be okay. Not wanting or worrying, not anxious or stressed. If only we could bottle it. For those of us who know the grief of a marriage breakdown and understand the fear of the future, we know that it's hard to feel okay. It has seemed so far away for a long time. At some stages, it seems impossible that we will ever feel okay again. Letting go of grief is a process, but taking the steps you need to help yourself will get you there. Just take one step at a time. Put the effort into one small step and take it slow. You'll get there ... and it's so worth it.

# 10

## A SUMMARY

### You're Not Alone

Unfortunately, my experience of hurt, trauma, a difficult marriage, and a legal battle is not unique. Many men and women have gone through similar struggles for decades. My belief that things must change has given me the push to write about this topic that I know all too well. Divorce should be dealt with differently for everyone whose relationship has broken down. Feeling alone on our journeys is unhealthy and makes things more difficult. I have chosen to share my experience to highlight the realities of relationship breakdown and divorce.

### Understanding Our Legal Rights

As citizens who are not legal experts, we often don't give it a second thought when we do things that involve legal contracts.

### Small Agreements

Examples include making a purchase in a shop or employing someone to provide a service, such as a haircut, having the bathroom tiled, or getting a gate hung. All of these examples involve contracts.

## Big Agreements

There is a contract in place when we take out a bank loan. Such contracts involve a lot more work from us. No lending institute will entertain us unless they know a lot about us, such as our employment details and financial history. If we're not good for what we say we are, no contract will be given.

On the scale of important agreements, where does the agreement to marry another person come into play? Does anyone even think about it as a legal contract? Should we? What are the requirements?

Technically, there are a few basic requirements: you must be over the age of 18, have the mental capacity to marry, not be related by blood, and freely consent to the marriage. You must also observe the necessary marriage formalities, give notice to the registrar or church, and be either single, widowed, or divorced. These things considered, there is definitely something missing from this list of requirements to marry in Ireland. The Catholic Church's pre-marriage courses, perhaps? In fairness, I know lots of couples who were encouraged to attend these courses by their priest, who was very helpful with his advice on marriage! Okay, that may be slightly facetious and unhelpful but, from where I'm standing, pre-marriage courses run by the Church are not the answer.

Prior to engaging in a legally binding marriage contract, should we be informed of what this entails? Would this remove the romantic desire for everlasting love? Should being informed on this be optional or a requirement? In my view, yes, we should be informed on such an important contract. I don't want to remove any romance – I love a bit of romance! However, the realities of divorce can be horrific, as can the realisation that property is treated as a marital asset, even if you purchased it long before you got married. Have the difficult conversations, become informed, and understand that you can still live happily ever after.

### MEDIATION: A PROFESSION

A profession is a field of work that has been successfully professionalised. It can be defined as a disciplined group of individual professionals, who adhere to ethical standards and who hold themselves out as – and are accepted by the public as – possessing special knowledge and skills in a widely recognised body of learning derived from research, education, and training at a high level, and who are prepared to apply this knowledge and exercise these skills in the interest of others.

In my experience, mediation has been greatly undermined by family law professionals. Unfortunately, clients of mine and of colleagues have been strongly dissuaded from using mediation to create the terms of their agreement. Clients are regularly advised against mediation by solicitors in what is apparently their best interests. It is understandable that some people do, for example, refuse to negotiate or neglect to prioritise the best interests of their children, and those people should really be in front of a judge. When people attend mediation with an experienced mediator, such outcomes are not typically the case.

Mediation works to break down the barriers caused by conflict and set the scene for a workable agreement between the parties. In my opinion, it is not in the best interests of a client when a solicitor advises them against mediation.

Mediation is indeed a profession. For me, it is also a passion, and for many talented mediators, an artform. For separating and divorcing couples, mediation is the future: it is the way forward in dealing with hurt, anger, and trauma. It is the progressive way to deal with parenting and finances.

Knowledge is power. Understanding what professional mediation can achieve will change the landscape of how we deal with divorce.

- Mediation is recognised in law by the Mediation Act 2017.
- Mediation can provide legally-binding separation agreements without the need to attend court.
- Mediation is suitable for highly acrimonious disputes.
- Mediation works effectively for all value cases, including High Court cases.
- Mediation for separating couples is encouraged and supported by judges throughout Ireland.
- Mediation allows for full disclosure of marital assets.
- Mediation enables effective parenting after divorce.
- Mediated agreements can be used for consent-based divorces.

## UNDERSTANDING THE TRADITIONAL SYSTEM OF DIVORCE

The traditional route to divorce through solicitors and barristers will always be there. This is absolutely necessary – just not for the majority of people. For various reasons, some people are simply convinced that, through this route, they will receive justice for hurt, or in some way redeem their good name.

Others are guided by solicitors, who still protest that they need full disclosure to advise their clients. They often tell their clients that, unless they go to court, this disclosure cannot be achieved. A word of caution: disclosure and further discovery are extremely lengthy and expensive processes in court, and there is no guarantee that the suspected missing money will be found. On occasion, the money that we expected to locate through the discovery process is gone, and we often have no recourse. This has been my experience, in any case.

What is the point of all this disclosure and documentation if not to allow full transparency? Can assets be taken and removed without proper explanation? In my experience, the answer is yes, one hundred percent: money and assets can be removed. The mechanism advised by my solicitors didn't work and no explanation was offered. Rest assured that, if this happened to me, it also happens to many others. The advice I received regarding finding the missing money and assets was expensive. Like the whole experience of court, the only thing you're guaranteed at the end is a large bill. This is not to say that discovery and forensic accountancy do not work in some cases – I'm sure they do. However, the process is uncertain, expensive, and arduous, to say the least. Surely any sensible person would prefer an alternative process.

When sense does not prevail, and parents decide not to pay maintenance or put their children first, these cases will require the ruling of a judge. Unfortunately, however, we appear to be unable to achieve any real guidelines as to what correct provision actually looks like. Again and again, we are told that it depends on the judge, it depends on the day, some judges like men, others like women. In my experience, judges do their best to offer fairness. My honest belief is that many solicitors say that it depends on the judge because they simply don't know what to advise.

## A REALITY CHECK

There was a day not so long ago when I saw nine clients, which is not typical. There was a small administrative error, which led to a couple of extra clients being booked in so I worked late. Anyhow, I met nine people who each had their own story, some of which were full of heartbreak and frustration, while others had issues to discuss and plans to examine. By the end of that day, I was absolutely mentally and physically drained. Every ounce of my mental and emotional energy goes into helping people to alter their positions and create workable agreements.

Meanwhile, outside my window, I could see the courthouse, almost within touching distance. In the morning, I can see the crowds congregating outside. Some men and women are alone, while others have support. I see lots of solicitors bustling around and usually a few Gardaí going in and out. On the one or two days of the month on which family law cases are heard, there is only one judge – one judge at a time to preside over all the family law cases! *One* human being in that courthouse who is tasked with hearing your case. There could be seventy or eighty couples on the list! On what planet can that one judge be expected to hear what's important to you and your children? Of course, they will do their best to judge fairly, but you're in the wrong place if you want your feelings to be considered. This is simply not the right place for it. The courts are under tremendous pressure and are not serving divorcing couples well.

We could have ten judges in every courthouse in Ireland, five days of the week, but creating court battles out of broken marriages is not the best way to deal with marital breakdown and settling on the terms of a divorce. A court battle is unnecessary and, in my opinion, akin to using a sledgehammer to crack an egg.

Regardless of my personal beliefs, which I have formed after nearly two decades of dealing with the family courts, the overriding issue is that the system is broken. When going into court, the only thing you know is that you don't know anything for sure ... except that you'll receive a hefty bill.

## THE DIFFERENCE BETWEEN SOLICITORS, BARRISTERS, AND MEDIATORS

Let's be honest: when it comes to family law, the roles of solicitors, barristers, and mediators are very different. Linked, but different. I believe it is extremely important to address the significance of these roles, as well as the differences between them. Firstly, let's look at some of their pros and cons.

## Mediation: The Highlights

- Mediation works in the best interests of both parties, as well as their children.
- Mediation is recognised in law.
- Mediation can create legally binding separation agreements.
- Mediation deals with separations and divorces outside of the courtroom.
- Mediation helps create better future working relationships.
- Mediation is less costly.
- Mediation bodies require high ethical standards.
- Mediation is a self-determined process.
- Mediators do not side with either party.
- Parenting is managed.
- A determination of agreement can be reached and drafted in as little as two months.

## Solicitors and Barristers: The Highlights

- Solicitors and barristers can act for those who do not meet the criteria for mediation.
- They are best placed to act in cases where criminal allegations have been made.
- Services are expensive: the cost of divorce in Ireland is typically around €30,000.
- The process is lengthy: achieving a separation in Ireland can take anywhere from twelve months to many years.
- Many people find the process of the legal system to be extremely unclear.

- The courts are unfamiliar, the traditional system is void of empathy, and the experience is extremely upsetting for many people.
- Solicitors can only act for one party and against the other, which can cause further trauma to the parties and children involved in the marriage breakup.
- Establishing the highlights of these roles will help to determine the differences between them. However, there is a lack of clarity for many people, as they are unfamiliar with the different routes to divorce and how they work. The principal (and most relevant) difference is that solicitors and barristers only work for one side, whereas your mediator works for both parties. The nature of the legal route is divisive (which, in my experience, is putting it mildly), whilst the mediation route works for both halves of the separated couple.

## OUR CHILDREN

We need to get divorce right, not just for ourselves, but for our children. 95 per cent of mediation clients cite the wellbeing of their children as their number one issue of importance, and this is where the vast majority of my clients wish to begin. Couples naturally want what's best for their children. Deep down, they know what's right, but there is often a lot of hurt and pain to deal with, which can be intertwined with what's best for the children. When you're feeling pain, it's hard to always make the right choices, so it's vital not to further exacerbate that pain. We need to be able to focus on the best interests of our children.

Have you ever heard the phrase, 'Children are resilient'? I have, I just don't believe it to be true; it never sat well with me. Studies show that it is unlikely that our children have natural resilience. Perhaps you have heard the phrase, 'Children are like sponges.' Well, that one makes sense to me. If the latter is true, shouldn't we be extremely mindful of what they soak up? To a large extent, our children feel what we feel. Their wellbeing is largely determined by how they are nurtured and loved. We can do our best to shield them, but how we deal with divorce and separation will most definitely have a lasting effect on our children.

Parenting through divorce is difficult. Don't make it more difficult than it has to be. Try putting a few practical tips in place to help yourself through this tough time, and if at all possible, avoid a court-room battle.

## THE POWER OF SOCIETY

Our society is unrecognisable since we campaigned in the streets in 1986. Since then, we have made so much progress. It is therefore hard to believe that some of the same barriers to divorce that existed in the late 1980s are still in place today.

The biggest changes in the world came about with the movement of society. Though the conversation about divorce – and how it affects us and our children – has started, I don't believe there is enough understanding of the negative impact of a difficult, embittered court battle on top of a heartbreaking split. Our mental health services are at breaking point. More than ever before, we understand what stress can do to our mental health and wellbeing. We understand anxiety and we know that medications are available. In the aftermath of a nasty, solicitor-led divorce, do we really want to be treated with medication for years to come? When our loved ones, friends, and colleagues are dealing with the hurt and trauma of a marriage split, it can be hard to see the wood for the trees. The current system is simply unsuitable for most people seeking a divorce, and its mental health impact upon our children is yet to be quantified. The stress caused to families and children is as clear as day. The most common route to divorce is an outdated practice but there is a better alternative. We can make a positive change that benefits our children by encouraging our friends and families to avoid a court battle where at all possible.

For these reasons, I strongly believe it is important that we are all informed about this issue. The support we need isn't about getting the best solicitor or throwing money at a system that will not offer relief from hurt. Divorce does not have to be so difficult. The more we understand, the more we can help our friends, families, and others in society.

## OUR GOVERNMENT

In previous chapters, I have addressed the acknowledgement from government that there are many failings in the current court system, and you will have read that there are many plans to attempt to improve them. Unfortunately, this is simply not enough. Many families urgently need to achieve divorce without outrageous costs and extensive waiting lists. In reality, the government could drastically improve this situation far more easily than many of our other crises. There are no easy solutions to the housing and healthcare catastrophes in this country, but the divorce system is an issue which can be fixed.

The government appears to be primarily focused on increasing the capacity of the courts to shuffle through thousands of split-up couples, enabling solicitors and barristers to continue leading our divorces. Although there is acknowledgment of and support for mediation, more needs to be done. Reform is required, but not in the millions or billions. A conversation is needed with someone whose interests do not lie in preserving the traditional route to divorce. The stakeholders in these discussions to find a solution must be neutral and have no vested interest in preserving the current system. Countries such as Switzerland enable their citizens to achieve a divorce through a few emails!

Should the government examine the legal costs paid by divorcing couples and address why they are so high? I believe the costliest aspect of a divorce is the decision-making process for establishing correct provision. There is simply a better way to deal with this than bargaining on the steps of the court. More extensive guidelines from the courts as to what correct provision looks like would be one such improvement. Though every case is different, it is ridiculous to leave it to 'horse trading' or the humour of the judge on the day. It's time things changed.

It is simply unacceptable that the average wage earner in this country needs to come up with €30,000 (and often much more) to avail of their legal right to divorce. It's not rocket science. Adjustments to legislation and an awareness campaign to inform Irish citizens would all be very achievable. I'm available for the discussion.

## SELF-CARE

Getting through life, let alone divorce, creates challenge after challenge. There are so many factors that influence how we cope, thrive, fall down, and get back up. We all have different backgrounds and upbringings, which colour our coping mechanisms. My generation and the generations before were reared with the sayings: 'You'll be grand,' 'No crying,' 'Hit them back,' and 'Hit them harder.' We were taught to ignore someone who was not nice. Many of us learned few conflict resolution skills, so it's unsurprising that looking after ourselves is such a foreign concept. This is definitely changing. Human beings desire to improve life for future generations, and we do this by teaching our children and striving to do our best.

## Remember to Breathe

The tools, tips, and tricks for self-care can be hard to engage during times of serious stress. So don't – just breathe. Breathe deep and slow. Catch your thoughts. Slow things down, watch your thoughts go by. Give yourself a moment or two. Don't react. Recognise that you're dealing with stress and make the decision not to react now.

Just breathe.

The thoughts are stressful. You may have any number of problems with ex-spouses, solicitors, or bills, all of which may be out of your control. One thing you can control are your thoughts. Learning to control these is like learning to use a muscle. No amount of panic or anxiety can change the wording of the letter or text, or whatever else is causing the stress, but you can control your thoughts. So, breathe slower and give yourself two minutes where you don't react. Maybe two minutes won't do it – I know I've had times where I've had to take hours. You can build a muscle if you repeatedly lift the weight. Likewise, if you keep up the practice of not reacting, just breathing, and work on your thoughts, you can train your brain.

## Sleep

Dealing with stress goes hand-in-hand with looking after ourselves. There is a combination of factors involved in training our brains and bodies to deal with the tough situations that life brings. Sleep is a key component. Put the effort into making sure you get the correct sleep. Follow the sleep routine recommended by experts, try every natural remedy going, drink the chamomile, take the magnesium, turn off the technology, and read the book to give yourself every chance of getting a good night's sleep. Be kind to yourself.

## Diet

It's the most natural thing in the world to want to comfort ourselves through times of stress and heartbreak. I for one have used every comfort food on the menu, as well as copious amounts of wine. This is to a point: it mustn't become the norm or an everyday occurrence. By all means, have a blowout: eat the ice-cream and have a weekend under the duvet – have two! But also give yourself the advice you'd offer to your sister or best friend. You need to get yourself the best help available. Looking after your diet will help to clear your head and give you the energy you need, now more than ever. I know you're not training for the Olympics but you're going through stress and trauma, something you weren't expecting. You will need your health to embrace your new life.

## Exercise

Endorphins – you need them now. No, you can't buy them. You make them, or rather your body releases them during exercise. What will they do? They'll make you feel good, better than the ice-cream (though maybe not immediately). They are free and available at any time. You'll never regret getting them. Others can get them with you and they will feel the benefits of you having them. You'll be better company for yourself and it will therefore be easier to love yourself, which you're going to start doing. Do it! Go on, you know you want to.

Serotonin is a chemical that carries messages between nerve cells in the brain and throughout your body, playing a key role in bodily functions such as mood, sleep, and digestion. This is the chemical that helps stave off depression and we can help to produce it through exercise. There is much research into the causes and treatment of depression to support the link between the production of serotonin and brain health. All in all, there is nothing to lose and everything to gain when it comes to getting our daily exercise in whatever form that may take.

## BE BRAVE

Letting go can be hard but it's so worth it. Take the steps to start your next chapter. Be brave, be bold, be better.

# A MISSION STATEMENT

The time has come to make a change to how we divorce in Ireland.

In divorcing our once cherished partners, we are fracturing connections that were once designed to last a lifetime. These connections were our lifeline for love, our support systems, our whole lives. The pain of the break is searing, the connection that has been severed is an emotional, physical, mental and often financial loss. It is a loss that is impossible to quantify on paper or in a court of law. A person or even a number of people whom you had relied upon, who you believed were there for you, who had been your family, have evaporated from your life. Not always entirely gone, but their role has changed. It can be overwhelming sense of loss for many.

As a society we are judging our divorcees, as a government we have approved a torturous broken system to deal with divorce. Our legal system has, by and large, become seemingly immune to emotional pain.

It is all our responsibility to look after each other. To recognise pain in the trauma of divorce and separation. We must protect our children; we must do what is best for those who are hurting and who need help.

We can all do more to understand conflict, to discuss and understand how we personally deal with hurt and trauma. We have been telling ourselves and others 'we're fine' for far too long. Accepting that it is natural to respond to our world falling apart (through divorce) by way of a 'fight or flight' reaction, and knowing what that looks like, is the way forward. Knowing and accepting the need to support individuals, not persecute them, is essential. It is key to human compassion.

Divorcing with clearer legislation is also key. The government has a responsibility to advise us what correct provision looks like. What the 'division of assets' really means, what marital assets are. They must provide a clearer guide to what maintenance for children and spouses should look like. These are not straightforward requests; however with clearer guides it will greatly reduce the need for highly contested divorces and lengthy court cases. The idea that discovering 'correct provision' or entitlement to maintenance is a mystery that can only be solved by way of traditional route to divorce in Ireland must become a bygone practice.

We must acknowledge that the benefit of clarity on these issues will greatly outweigh any possible drawbacks. The government should allow a process of this very necessary improvement in legislation around how we divorce to be led by those who do not have a vested interest in continuing the current mechanism for achieving divorce. This is key to improving how we divorce. Currently, it appears that those in the legal profession greatly influence any decisions on reform of divorce. Surely they cannot be expected to make decisions that will inevitably take away court cases and reduce billable hours for their colleagues. For me, the current situation where legal bodies have a major voice in any reform is akin to having the CEOs of the tobacco industry make decisions on the distribution of cigarettes.

Government must take responsibility for the people of Ireland and allow for easier, more accessible divorce. This in my view does looks very different to the practices of the past twenty-five years.

Prenuptial agreements are, in my view, also key to moving away from acrimonious divorces. Legislation must be provided for these. Accepting that divorce is here, and that our system to divorce needs an overhaul, must include legislative reform to allow for prenuptial and post-nuptial agreements. I would like to see drafting of legislation to allow consenting adults legalise agreements to cater for the event that they separate.

My hope is with greater understanding and awareness that we all know without any doubt that barristers and solicitors are not the best route to a fair agreement between separating couples. I would like to see that the practice of employing a professional mediator as the way forward for the vast majority of separations and divorces in Ireland.

I would also like to see a time where cases taken to the courts are clearly unusual and definitely in the minority. That the only court cases taken by solicitors and barristers are those with criminal aspects. That because of this sea change in how we as a society deal with our divorces the courts have the time to consider these acrimonious cases in a timely fashion.

I would like to see a scenario where the vast majority of informed, reasonable people arrive at court with a separation agreement made outside of the courtroom. That their experience in court is only to achieve their consent divorce.

I would like to see a time where we can talk about the way we used to divorce – until we knew better!